in East Yorkshire

by
John and Nancy Eckersley

with
Mark Comer
and
Daniel Savage

© and published by
John E. Eckersley 2010

ISBN 978-0 9535862 5-7

Printed by
The Max Design & Print Co., York, England

FOREWORD
by David Neave

WITH ITS COMFORTABLE TERRAIN, well-marked rights of way, many quiet roads with broad verges, and a rich natural and man-made heritage, East Yorkshire is a leisure walker's paradise, but it is relatively unknown. Here, in a most original way, John and Nancy Eckersley have devised 26 walks, from Arras to the Zigzag Plantation, that explore the region's contrasting and delightful landscapes. These range from the low-lying meadows along the River Derwent, through the steep-sided dry valleys of the Wolds, to the dramatic chalk cliffs at Bempton and the sandy beaches of Spurn Point.

The route descriptions are accompanied by clear maps, photographs and detailed information on features of special interest. There is much to see along the walks: ancient woodland and wild flower meadows, great colonies of sea birds and wild fowl, prehistoric earthworks and lost village sites. Some of the East Riding's most historic villages are visited: Rudston with its Neolithic standing stone, Bishop Wilton and the site of the Archbishop of York's 'palace', and North Newbald with a splendid Norman church. On all except one walk there is at least one historic church, ranging from the charming small isolated rural churches at Great Givendale and Speeton to the great medieval town churches of Hedon and Howden. Some are open and for almost all a key is available nearby and worth chasing up. With forward planning a walk can be combined with a visit to one of the stately homes en route, Burton Agnes and Wassand, or one of the fascinating small museums at Bridlington, Hedon, Hornsea and Withernsea.

I am very pleased to commend this well-researched and well-presented book that will introduce many to the hidden treasures of East Yorkshire. John Eckersley is to be praised for the hours of research and writing and I hope not too arduous walks he has undertaken to produce yet another publication from which the profits will go to support the work of Christian Aid.

David Neave

Former Senior Lecturer at the University of Hull

Researcher, writer and lecturer on the history, landscape and buildings of East Yorkshire for over forty years.

LETTER FROM WETWANG

I F THERE WERE EVER a national competition to find the country's most fabulous sounding place names, there's no doubt that Yorkshire would win hands down. Whip Ma Whop Ma Gate in York, The Land of Green Ginger in Hull and Ugglebarnby on The North York Moors would all be contenders but the East Riding has got its own superb selection.

The trouble is, when you grow up accustomed to local curiosities, you take them for granted and you forget how wonderful they might be to outsiders. So, imagine you are a young child, coming from somewhere less blessed than Yorkshire, and you are told that for the first time you're going to visit Fridaythorpe or Thorngumbald or Uncleby. You'd be spellbound with enchantment!

John Eckersley has searched through his maps and wandered all over the county to find some unforgettable places. His wife, Nancy, has taken some fine photos of East Riding hidden treasure. At the same time they have devised an Alphabet Trail to make up an 'A to Z' of East Yorkshire. Who would ever have thought that there was a 'Q' or an 'X' or a 'Z' place to visit?

Have fun as you walk and search for gems in East Yorkshire but just remember one thing: if there's sea fret at Bridlington, snow storms on the High Wolds or mist in the Vale of York, it's nothing to do with me!

Paul Hudson

**BBC Look North Television Weather Forecaster
and Honorary Mayor of Wetwang**

(which place, of course, gets the Weatherman's Gold Medal in the Most Wonderful Village Name Competition)

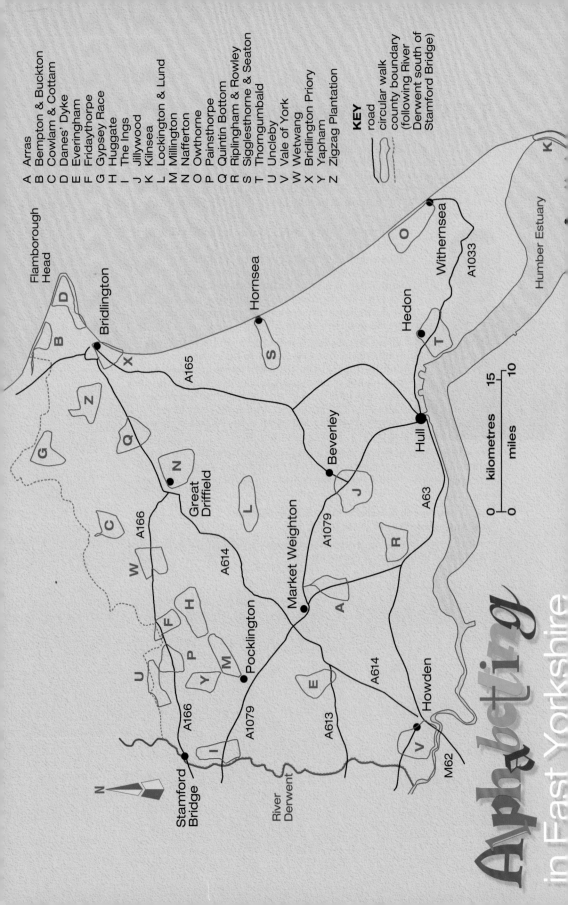

Alphabeting

in East Yorkshire

A Arras
B Bempton & Buckton
C Cowlam & Cottam
D Danes' Dyke
E Everingham
F Fridaythorpe
G Gypsey Race
H Huggate
I The Ings
J Jillywood
K Kilnsea
L Lockington & Lund
M Millington
N Nafferton
O Owthorne
P Painsthorpe
Q Quintin Bottom
R Riplingham & Rowley
S Sigglesthorne & Seaton
T Thorngumbald
U Uncleby
V Vale of York
W Wetwang
X Bridlington Priory
Y Yapham
Z Zigzag Plantation

KEY
— road
⬭ circular walk
---- county boundary
(following River
Derwent south of
Stamford Bridge)

N

Flamborough
Head

Bridlington

Hornsea

Withernsea

Hedon

Hull

Beverley

Great
Driffield

Market Weighton

Pocklington

Stamford
Bridge

Howden

River
Derwent

Humber Estuary

A165
A166
A1079
A614
A613
A63
A1033
M62

0   5   10   15   kilometres
0   5   10   miles

ALPHABETTING IN EAST YORKSHIRE

WALK	LOCATION	OS MAP (EXPLORER)	START	DISTANCE (miles approx)
A	ARRAS	293	Arras (A1079)	10.5
B	BEMPTON & BUCKTON	301	Speeton	10.9
C	COWLAM & COTTAM	300	Cowlam	8.8
D	DANES' DYKE	301	Flamborough	11.2
E	EVERINGHAM	294 & 291	Seaton Ross	9.6
F	FRIDAYTHORPE	294	Fridaythorpe	8.0
G	GYPSEY RACE	301	Burton Fleming	11.5
H	HUGGATE	294	Huggate	9.1
I	The INGS	294	Wilberfoss	9.2
J	JILLYWOOD LANE	293	Walkington	11.8
K	KILNSEA	292	Kilnsea	8.9
L	LOCKINGTON & LUND	294 & 295	Lockington	9.9
M	MILLINGTON	294	Millington	9.9
N	NAFFERTON	295	Driffield	9.9
O	OWTHORNE	292	Withernsea	11.4
P	PAINSTHORPE	294	Wayrham (A166)	8.9
Q	QUINTIN BOTTOM	295	Burton Agnes	9.7
R	RIPLINGHAM & ROWLEY	293	Brantingham	10.8
S	SIGGLESTHORNE	295	Sigglesthorne	9.3
T	THORNGUMBALD	292 & 293	Thorngumbald	11.7
U	UNCLEBY	294	Kirby Underdale	9.7
V	VALE OF YORK	291	Howden	10.1
W	WETWANG	294 & 300	Wetwang	10.2
X	X MARKS THE SPOT	295	Bridlington	7.9
Y	YAPHAM	294	Yapham	8.9
Z	ZIGZAG PLANTATION	301	Boynton	10.0

In 1974 controversial local government reorganisation left the historic county of the East Riding with considerably less territory than previously. In the north large parts of the Wolds and the Vale of Pickering went to North Yorkshire and in the west the land between the Rivers Derwent and Ouse also changed administration. The city of Hull is today a Unitary Authority separate from the East Riding. 'The old East Riding' in this book refers to the county as it existed before 1974.

In 'Alphabetting in East Yorkshire' the selection of walks has been intentionally restricted to the present East Riding. This has meant that some very interesting places, such as Wharram Percy and Kirby Grindalythe from the older, larger, East Riding have had to be omitted. Other historic villages such as Goodmanham and Londesborough, as well as the market towns of Beverley, Market Weighton and Pocklington, have been excluded because they were all represented in our previous walking book, 'Wilberforce Way'.

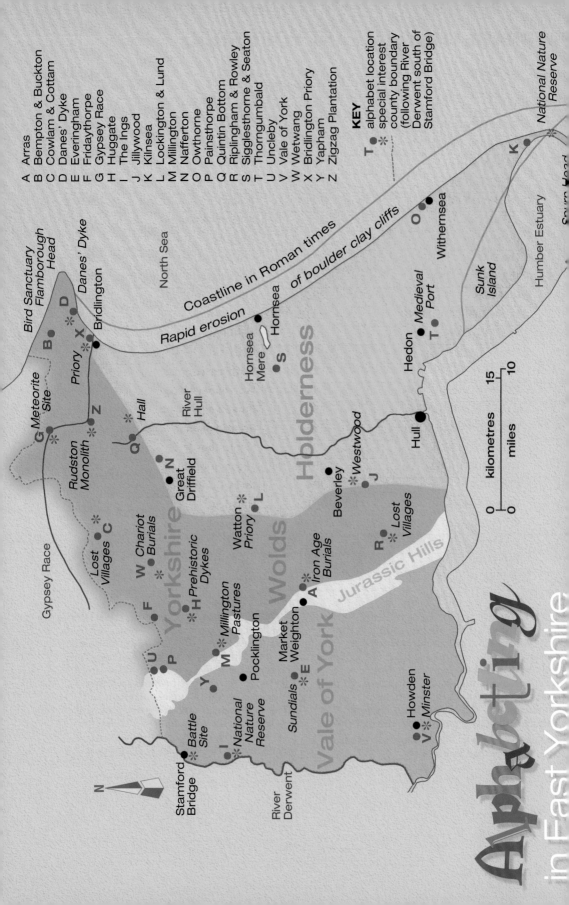

Alphabeting
in East Yorkshire

KEY

A Arras
B Bempton & Buckton
C Cowlam & Cottam
D Danes' Dyke
E Everingham
F Fridaythorpe
G Gypsey Race
H Huggate
I The Ings
J Jillywood
K Kilnsea
L Lockington & Lund
M Millington
N Nafferton
O Owthorne
P Painsthorpe
Q Quintin Bottom
R Riplingham & Rowley
S Sigglesthorne & Seaton
T Thorngumbald
U Uncleby
V Vale of York
W Wetwang
X Bridlington Priory
Y Yapham
Z Zigzag Plantation

T alphabet location
✳ special interest
      county boundary
      (following River
      Derwent south of
      Stamford Bridge)

National Nature
Reserve

North Sea

Coastline in Roman times

Rapid erosion   of boulder clay cliffs

Bird Sanctuary
Flamborough
Head

Danes' Dyke

Bridlington

Priory

Hornsea
Mere

Hornsea

Holderness

Meteorite
Site

Rudston
Monolith

Hall

River
Hull

Westwood

Beverley

Gypsey Race

Lost
Villages

Great
Driffield

Watton
Priory

Wolds

Yorkshire

Chariot
Burials

Prehistoric
Dykes

Millington
Pastures

Lost
Villages

Jurassic Hills

Medieval
Port

Withernsea

Hedon

Hull

Sunk
Island

Humber Estuary

Spurn Head

Iron Age
Burials

Market
Weighton

Pocklington

Sundials

Vale of York

Howden

Minster

Stamford
Bridge

Battle
Site

National
Nature
Reserve

River
Derwent

N

0   kilometres   15
0   miles   10

LANDSCAPES

Four different areas can be identified in the East Riding of Yorkshire and each has its own distinctive landscape characteristics. All four areas are represented on different walks in this book. The Vale of Pickering lies north of the region and part of this lowland used to be included within the East Riding but since the re-defining of county boundaries in 1974 the Vale of Pickering is now part of North Yorkshire.

The Vale of York extends to the western part of East Yorkshire where it is drained by the River Derwent as it flows south to join the Ouse at Barmby. Land is generally below 15m with much of the area covered with a mantle of varied glacial materials. These were either dumped by the glacier that moved south down the Vale in the Ice Age or were washed out from it by meltwater streams. However, two ridges of material known as the York and Escrick moraines lie across the lowland and mark the places where the ice stood stationary for long periods. These moraines stand higher than the surrounding land and since prehistoric times have provided routeways across the marshy Vale as well as giving sites for settlements. Holme Hill is the only other significant raised point in the Vale. Flooding along the Derwent is still a regular problem although the barrage at Barmby now stops salt water from the tidal River Ouse entering the Derwent.

Jurassic Hills Between the Vale of York and the Wolds lies a belt of Jurassic rocks that form a distinctive stretch of countryside. This band of rocks widens out towards the north where the limestones and sandstones have been dissected by surface streams and form low hills about 30-60m high. Good building stone and springs at the foot of the chalk Wolds were advantages for village settlement in places like Brantingham and North and South Cliffe.

The Wolds form the heartland of the region and are an arc of chalk hills stretching from the Humber estuary to the spectacular cliffs at Flamborough Head. One writer in 1586 called them 'a heap of mountains' but their highest point is only 246m at Garrowby Hill. They form gently rolling countryside and are characterised by their networks of steep-sided dry valleys. Thixendale, at the focus of six valleys, has an especially attractive location. It is generally believed that the valleys were cut by meltwater at the end of the Ice Age but then, when the frozen ground thawed, surface water could sink into the permeable chalk rock below, leaving the valleys dry. Today only the Gypsey Race in the Great Wold Valley can be classed as a permanent stream.

Rather surprisingly, the Yorkshire Wolds are not a designated Area of Outstanding Natural Beauty (AONB) even though the Lincolnshire Wolds are given this official classification.

Holderness lies to the east of the Wolds and is covered with a variety of glacial and post-glacial deposits lying on top of the eastward dipping chalk. The low, hummocky boulder clay ('till') used to contain numerous lakes in its marshy hollows but only Hornsea Mere remains today. It is Yorkshire's biggest natural lake.

Along the coastline, the boulder clay cliffs rise to a maximum of 38m but they have been eroded at an alarming rate and numerous villages have been lost to the sea. However, at the end of the coastline, the sea has built up the long sand and shingle spit of Spurn Head, formed from the materials eroded from further north and transported down the coast by longshore drift.

Inland, the River Hull and a network of dikes now drain the flat alluvial and peat-covered lands through which the river flows. Towards the north there used to be much marshy 'carr' land that restricted settlement whilst to the south the wide expanse of silt land has been largely built over as the city of Hull has expanded. Nevertheless, in 2007 serious flooding in Hull was a reminder of the vulnerability of concrete and tarmac landscapes to prolonged periods of heavy rain.

Further to the east, the zone of reclaimed land continues along the shore of the Humber estuary where Sunk Island – a strange name for an area that has arisen from out of the sea – adds an area of dead flat land to East Yorkshire.

PLACE NAMES

After the departure of the Romans from Britain around 400 AD, East Yorkshire saw Anglian invaders come and settle in East Yorkshire, entering either via Flamborough Head or the Humber Estuary.

The earliest Anglian settlement names are believed to be those ending in '*-ing*', '*-ingham*' or '*-ham*' ('homestead'). For example, in the area around Goodmanham (Bede recorded it as 'Godmundingaham') we find Everingham, Brantingham and Riplingham.

From their first sites, the Angles later moved out to almost all other parts of East Yorkshire and we can identify these villages by their '*-ton*' or '*-ington*' ('farmstead') names. By the time of the Domesday Survey (1086) nearly 300 of the 440 settlements in the old East Riding had Anglian names of one sort or another.

When the Danes (Vikings) captured the Anglian town of York in 867 AD and established their rule for nearly 100 years, they left their imprint on the place name geography of the region. Sometimes they settled in existing Anglian villages and just changed the names into what are known as 'hybrid' names. Nearly 70 hybrid or Scandinavianised names have been recognised in the old East Riding.

In other cases the Danes established new villages and the earlier ones are often identified by names ending in '*-by*' ('farm'). Later sites have '*-thorpe*' as their endings. A 'thorpe' settlement was a secondary outlying hamlet away from the original settlement. Other Scandinavian name endings include '*-wick*' (dairy farm), '*-holm*' and '*-carr*' indicating marshy areas.

There are about 40 '*-by*', 70 '*-thorpe*' and 40 other Scandinavian names in the old East Riding. Together with the hybrids this gives a total of some 220 Scandinavian names.

Settlements that have purely Scandinavian names usually occupy relatively poorer land with less attractive soils because the Anglians had already taken the better areas. Around Bubwith, for example, the Angles had settled the lighter, sandy and gravelly soils and the heavier clays were left for the Danes, with their '*-by*' and '*-thorpe*' villages, to colonise at a later date.

'... any similarity or resemblance to persons known or unknown is entirely intentional...' (NE)

EAST YORKSHIRE / A BRIEF HISTORY

On, or close to, the routes of the 26 walks in this book we see many features that give us glimpses of the history of East Yorkshire.

Although there is only limited material from Paleolithic and Mesolithic times, East Yorkshire has abundant evidence of Neolithic (New Stone Age) activity. The **Neolithic Age** was a time of agricultural revolution when settled farming gradually replaced nomadic hunting and gathering economies. Earthworks such as the Willy Howe burial barrow and monuments like the Rudston standing stone are indications of the change in lifestyle.

As the Neolithic merged with the **Bronze Age**, huge dykes were constructed to define tribal territories and although many of these have been ploughed out and other features grown over, it is remarkable that so many can still be seen in the Wolds landscape.

Bronze was replaced by iron as a metal for agricultural and military use and in the **Iron Age** East Yorkshire was populated by the Parisi tribe, believed to have migrated from their centre in the Paris Basin area of northern France. Aspects of their occupation are recorded at the internationally significant cemetery sites of Arras and Wetwang. It is clear that theirs was a sophisticated society before it was submerged or assimilated with the new culture that arrived with the Romans.

Although we do not see **Roman** remains on the Alphabet Walks, mosaics from Roman villas at Brantingham and Rudston have been rescued and are on display in Hull Museums.

Anglian and **Scandinavian** colonisation of the countryside followed the decline of Roman authority and the place name evidence described on the previous page shows how widespread was the extent of their settlement. Anglo-Saxon Christian crosses can be seen at Lowthorpe and Holme-upon-Spalding-Moor.

After the defeat of the English by William the Conqueror in 1066, the old Anglo-Saxon order ended and during the ensuing **Norman** period huge changes took place in the English countryside. Especially important was the building of Norman Churches, large and small, and at Hedon a whole new town was laid out.

Not everything, of course, was positive. As the **medieval period** progressed, more and more inland villages became depopulated. The ridges and mounds we see on many of our walks are constant reminders of this.

East Yorkshire generally lacked industrial raw materials and so was spared some of the worst impacts of the Industrial Revolution in the 18th and 19th centuries. However, the **Georgian period** saw a wholesale transformation of the rural landscape largely through the actions of landed gentry such as the Sykes family of Sledmere. It was the landowners who instigated the enclosure of open arable fields, sheep walks and rabbit warrens and it was they who largely paid for the building of new farmsteads and the planting of hedgerows and woodlands. To them we also owe the legacy of landscaped parks and gardens like those at Houghton.

There were changes, too, in the villages. Sir Tatton Sykes I and even more his son, Sir Tatton Sykes II, were responsible for an astonishing programme of church building and restoration that they financed in the 19th and early 20th centuries. The old East Riding, however, was an important area of Non-conformism and over a hundred villages had both Wesleyan and Primitive Methodist chapels. Evidence of Victorian church building is clear on many Alphabet Walks.

The **Victorian** and **Edwardian** eras also brought important changes to the coast of East Yorkshire with Bridlington, Hornsea and Withernsea all seeking to benefit from the fledgling seaside tourist industry. Perhaps because of its richer maritime and ecclesiastical history, Bridlington fared better than her two smaller competitors, both of whom had unfortunate experiences with seaside pier building.

As a result of the 1974 local government **boundary changes**, the old East Riding has lost significant parts of its historic legacy. However, since then, archaeologists have continued to discover secrets of the past, farmers have been experimenting with new types of land use, redevelopment has brought at least some improvement to the seaside resorts, new museum and conservation groups have become active and tourism initiatives are now advertising the previously unheralded secrets of East Yorkshire. We hope your appetites have been whetted.

Approximate Early Timescale

Post 1066	**Medieval Britain**
AD 1066	Norman Conquest
	Vikings
	Anglo-Saxons
c. AD 455	Fall of Rome
	Roman Britain
AD 43	Roman Conquest
	Iron Age
c. 700 BC	End of Bronze Age
	Bronze Age
c. 2,000 BC	Beginning of Bronze Age
	Neolithic (New Stone) Age
c. 4,500 BC	Beginning of Neolithic Age
	Mesolithic (New Stone) Age
c. 8,000 BC	Beginning of Mesolithic Age
	Paleolithic (Old Stone) Age

WALK A
Arras

Map: Explorer 293 (and a little on 291)
S.E.P.: A1079 at Arras (926414)
Bus: X46 York-Hull
Longer walk distance: 10.5 miles
Shorter walk (uses bus or parked car to
return from N Newbald to Sancton): 6.0 miles
Special interest:
Arras Culture

We start from Arras itself (1), either having
alighted from the bus along the A1079 or having
parked our cars at the road junction. The
internationally important Iron Age cemetery lay
mainly to the north of the A1079 road at this
point although there is no information at the site
to tell us.

Crossing the A1079, we walk down
Hessleskew Lane and follow the
signs for the Wolds Way. Soon we

pass Arras Wold Farm and then Hessleskew before
the road swings right at (2). Here we leave the
tarmac and continue straight ahead on the Wolds
Way track to the end of the next large field at (3).

At this point we turn sharp right and take the
wide fieldside path that soon comes into a dry
valley and then twists for another mile or so along
the valley floor to the farm buildings at (4).
Turning left, we follow the left side of the hedge to
go up and over the spur before dropping fairly
steeply to North Newbald (5).

We go straight over the back road,
down the tarred alleyway
opposite and turn right

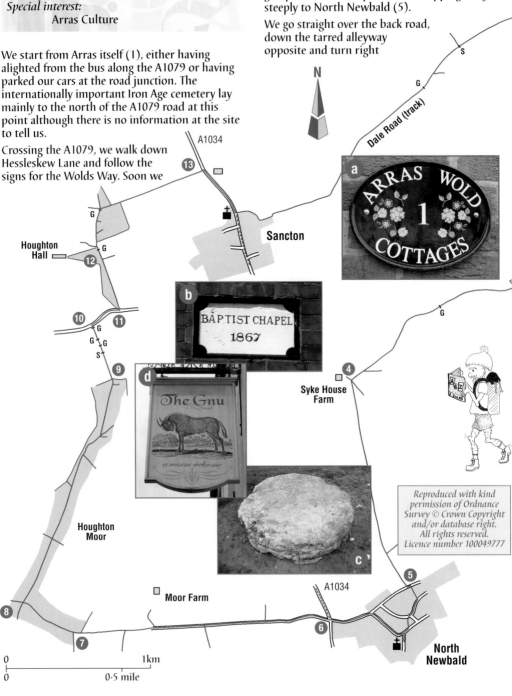

Reproduced with kind
permission of Ordnance
Survey © Crown Copyright
and/or database right.
All rights reserved.
Licence number 100049777

Arras

A1079 (1)

Arras Wold

Hessleskew

(2)

(3)

along Eastgate to the village green. We may wish to explore the village with its delightful limestone buildings but the walk continues round the green, past The Tiger and The Gnu pubs and on to St Nicholas Church on our left.

When we leave the churchyard by either of the gates on the east side, we turn left, left again on Burgate and then bend right on to Galegate. Soon the road curves left into Westgate and brings us to the A1034 at (6).

Even though the building is likely to be closed, we should make a point of seeing the octagonal tower, unique in East Yorkshire.

We leave the church using the path on to the A1034. Going directly across, we locate the bridleway opposite. This track, called

Dale Road, now leads us for two miles back to Hessleskew Lane. Twisting a little near the start, there is no problem following the route along the bottom of the dry valley. At first there are trees on either side with both blackthorn and hawthorn bushes. Later the path becomes open as we pass Noddles Hill on our way up to Hessleskew Lane. At the tarmac we turn left back to our start.

(From (8) a longer 11.8-mile walk goes straight on to the western edge of the woodland and follows fieldside paths before coming steeply down the narrow Jurassic limestone escarpment into North Cliffe.

In North Cliffe we turn right on the side road, join the main road and continue to the fingerpost next to a small orchard. We are directed back up to the top of the scarp face where we go left, then right and continue to the plank bridge over Witch Gill.

From here we go straight ahead down Cliffe Road. At first the lane is tarmacked but after the drive to Moor Farm (listen for the peacocks) it becomes an earthen track. As we enter the woods (7) we find a welcome change of environment. The track is well-maintained and shortly after we pass the isolated house called 'The Cottage' we come to the path crossing at (8).

Here we turn right and follow a wide, grassy track through the trees of Houghton Moor to the edge of the woods at (9). Towards the end of May the rhododendrons look superb. At the end of the trees the path bends left and continues along the side of the hedge to join Houghton Lane at (10).

Turning right, we walk as far as the fingerpost at (11) and here go left on the chalky track leading towards Houghton Hall.

Shortly after going through a gate, the main track swings left to the Hall but we bear right on the footpath (12). We walk to the left of the small wood and the drive to the Presbytery, turn sharp right at the kissing gate, go through the trees and then follow the wide grassy track to the A1034 road (13). A right turn brings us to All Saints Church, Sancton.

Across the stream, the OS map shows the p.r.o.w. lying on the right (SE) side of the hedge. However, access is virtually impossible at the time of writing and a well-trodden path lies on the left (NW) side. There is a wide margin left uncultivated as we carry on and turn right, then left, on the farm track to Castle Farm. Going through the farmyard, the track bends left and joins Houghton Lane close to where the shorter walk comes in at (10).)

Special Interest – Walk A

Arras 'the shielings' (shelters or huts)
Newbald 'the new building'
Sancton 'sand farm'
Hessleskew 'hazel wood'

Arras East Yorkshire is famous for its Iron Age burials and hundreds of graves have been excavated with many more still not investigated. The cemetery at **Arras** was first unearthed in 1815-17 and is acknowledged to be of international importance. Located a short distance from Arras, the burial area contained over 100 small barrows and is now split by the A1079 road. There is virtually nothing to see on the ground today.

Most of the barrows covered simple graves, with armlets, brooches and beads, although three were probably those belonging to chieftains, including one woman. These graves were more richly furnished. The 'King's Barrow' contained a man's body and the skeletons of two ponies and a wheeled cart or chariot. In the 'Queen's Barrow' was a woman wearing a glass necklace made of nearly 100 beads together with other bronze, amber and gold ornaments. A female with an iron mirror and the remains of another cart were found in the 'Lady's Barrow' whilst the 'Charioteer's Barrow' held a cart or chariot and part of a bronze shield. Such 'Chariot burials' are known elsewhere on the Wolds and especially at Wetwang (Walk **W**).

The 'Arras Culture' is known for the distinctive shape of its burial barrows – they are surrounded by square-plan ditches and so generally known as 'square barrows'. Although not usually visible to the naked eye at ground level, they can be detected as crop marks by aerial survey. There are, apparently, literally thousands of them in East Yorkshire.

Until recently chariot burials had been found only in the Yorkshire Wolds and the surrounding area but in 2001 a chariot grave was excavated at Newbridge near Edinburgh.

There are some similarities between the Yorkshire Arras burials and those found in the Champagne district of France. Moreover, the people living in East Yorkshire were called the Parisi and this was the name of the tribe that gave its name to Paris. So it is quite possible that the Arras Culture came from modern day France.

It is thought that the Arras Culture existed from around the 5th century BC to the time of the Roman invasion.

North Newbald is centred around its village green and the remains of its former cross. Four medieval roads, Burgate, Westgate, Galegate and Eastgate, radiate from this focus.

St Nicholas Church has been described as the most complete Norman Church in East Yorkshire and the four arches inside the building are especially well-preserved but unfortunately the church is likely to be closed during the week. North Newbald was owned by York Minster from the late 10th to the 19th centuries and this helps to explain the rich nature of the church building. As with numerous other buildings in the village, it is constructed from the local Jurassic limestone and this warm, sandy-coloured rock makes North Newbald unusually attractive.

All Saints Church, Sancton is known for its 15th century tower which is the only one in East Yorkshire that is octagonal from bottom to top. Next to the churchyard is a Roman Catholic cemetery with its own small memorial chapel and also close to the church is the site of an Anglo-Saxon burial ground. Several hundred burial urns, containing tweezers, combs and glass beads, were unearthed.

John Wesley preached in Sancton in 1788 and then got on his horse and went to speak at Market Weighton, Pocklington and York all on the same day. Not bad for an 85-year old.

The former **School** has an interesting history. An Anglican school, it was rebuilt in 1870 as a memorial to two local brothers, Thomas and Samuel Jackson, each of whom served as president of the Wesleyan Methodist Conference.

Houghton Hall, described by Pevsner & Neave as 'the perfect Georgian country house in a beautiful parkland setting', was built in the 1760s for the Roman Catholic landowner Philip Langdale. In the grounds is a large serpentine lake set at two levels and divided by a cascade.

Special Interest – Walk B

Bempton 'farm by a tree'

Buckton 'buck enclosure' (or personal name of Bucca is also possible)

Speeton 'speech enclosure' (probably the place where the Hundred met)

RSPB Bempton Cliffs are home to England's biggest seabird colony as well as the location of the largest population of breeding gannets on the UK mainland. Eight species nest here: gannets, guillemots, razorbills, puffins, kittiwakes, fulmars, herring gulls and shags and the five RSPB clifftop viewing points allow us to spot these in safety.

Snippets of interest from the RSPB leaflet inform us that:

Gannets have a wingspan as wide as an adult human armspan and they incubate their eggs under their feet;

Guillemots have dagger-shaped beaks and more slender necks than razorbills;

Razorbills, like the guillemots, do not build nests but lay their single egg on a bare rock ledge;

Puffins can carry as many as 64 fish in their bills and spend their winters out at sea;

Kittiwakes are a type of gull and get their name from their noisy, repetitive call;

Fulmars are related to albatrosses, pair for life and can live for up to 40 years;

Herring gulls, although in decline at Bempton, survive inland when they scavenge rubbish tips;

Shags nest in cliff caves near the tide line and, like cormorants, fly close to the water.

A total of 160 different species of bird have been recognised at the RSPB site since 1971.

'Climming' (climbing down the cliff-face on ropes to collect birds' eggs) was for centuries an important feature of the local economy, the eggs either being sold to collectors or eaten as part of the diet. Climmers worked the coast between Bempton and Speeton between May and September. A gang of four men (one collecting the eggs and the others controlling the ropes) could pick up to 400 eggs a day. Climming was declared illegal in 1954.

St Michael's Church, Bempton dates from the 13th century.

Buckton Hall stands a mile away from its village and was gutted by fire in 1919 so that the interior is no longer original. An inscription dated 1744/5 on one of the former beams declared that 'Ann Robinson is the prettiest girl in Yorkshire'.

St Leonard's Church, Speeton is one of the smallest parish churches in Yorkshire and dates from not later than 1100. Inside the church is a 12th century Agnus Dei carving (a lamb bearing a cross) and a Norman font.

After the Norman Conquest in 1066, most of Speeton parish eventually became part of the Bridlington Priory estates and the church relied on Bridlington for its administration.

During the 17th and 18th centuries the church survived with absentee curates and the fact that the building was so often empty has led to the suggestion that it may have been used as a storage depot by smugglers operating along the coast.

The lack of a burial ground meant that coffins used to be carried by the pall bearers to Bridlington Priory, a distance of some five miles.

St Leonard lived in the sixth century and, on account of his ministry to slaves and to felons, became the patron saint of prisoners.

WALK B
Bempton and Buckton

Map: Explorer 301
S.E.P.: St Leonard's Church, Speeton (151746)
Bus: 504 from Bridlington
'Balloon' walk distance: 10.9 miles
Shorter walk alternative: 5.6 miles
Special interest:
    RSPB Bempton

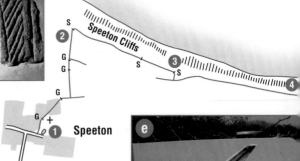

There are a number of possible variations to this walk but the description given below assumes that we start in Speeton (actually in North Yorkshire) and do a 'balloon' walk. This means we go east along the cliffs, complete a loop around Bempton and Buckton and then retrace our route to Speeton. A shorter alternative is to complete a 5.6 miles circuit around Bempton and Buckton only.

boulder clay before the path levels off and we get good views of Bridlington Bay ahead and the line of Danes' Dyke to our left.

We park in St Leonard's Church car park (1) at Speeton, note the rare Leicester Longwool sheep, and take the signed path towards the coast.

After the trees we cross diagonally over a field from one gate to another, we turn right, soon leave the track and turn sharp left at the fingerpost, go through two more gates and descend to the cliff edge at (2). Here we turn right and follow the Headland Heritage Coast path for some 3.7 miles.

Navigation is no problem. We turn steeply up the cliff slope at (3), cross from North into East Yorkshire (4), note the path to Hoddy Cows Lane (5) and as we approach Bempton RSPB centre the pace slows down as we stop at some of the viewing points to observe Bempton's bird life.

A path branching diagonally right leads to the RSPB building and toilets but the main walk continues along the cliff line for another 0.75 mile. Just after the Staple Newk viewing point, we turn inland at the red painted post (6) and take the recently created p.r.o.w. along the field boundary. We rise gently over the

FORMERLY
JAW BONES CORNER
TWO GIANT WHALE BONES MARKED THE ENTRANCE TO THIS FIELD

Going across the B1229, we visit St Michael's Church and, afterwards, we can use the seats by the village pond for a lunch break.

The walk carries on up Gillus Road before we turn left along the B1229 and continue on the pavement through Bempton and Buckton villages. Treasurer-hunters need to be watchful along this stretch of the walk!

At Hoddy Cows Lane (9) we turn right by a large pond and follow a wide hedged track towards the coast. Across to our left are the remains of ancient earthworks. Where the route turns sharp left (10), springs can make the ground a little boggy but otherwise the path is very attractive.

At the grassy track called Blakehowe Lane (7) we turn right and continue to Cliff Lane (8). Name-baggers note that to our right is Norway Farm, the pig breeding establishment that is called a 'multiplication unit'. Our route, however, turns left down the road and into Bempton.

When we come to the Headland Way path we turn left and retrace our steps to Speeton.

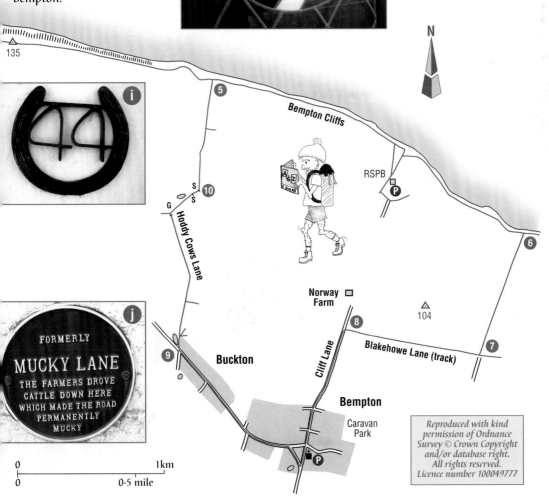

0 ——————————— 1km
0 ——————————— 0·5 mile

WALK C
Cowlam and Cottam

Map: Explorer 300
S.E.P.: St Mary's Church, Cowlam (965654)
Bus: No bus service
Longer walk distance: **8.3 miles**
Shorter walk alternative: **5.7 miles**
Special interest:
      Lost Villages

This walk visits the sites of the two lost villages of Cowlam and Cottam. Unfortunately there is no satisfactory bus connection. Car parking is possible on the grass verge by St Mary's Church, Cowlam and the route description starts from there.

From the road (1) we use the path through Church Farm to visit St Mary's Church. Although the church is normally closed, the key is available from the large white house adjacent to the church. A visit is well worthwhile, although we can still see the detailed carvings on the Norman font if we look through one of the windows.

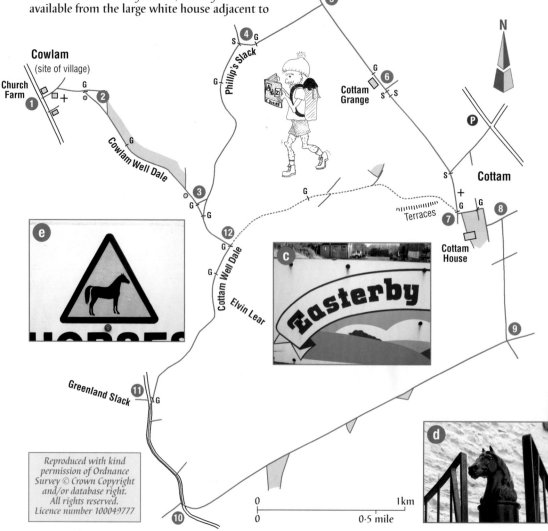

0   1km
0   0·5 mile

gate, across a horse paddock. We then follow the line of ET poles to Cottam's derelict church. The earthworks of the medieval village and the hollow-way between them are clearly visible.

From the church we carry on south for a short distance to the fingerpost and gate at (7). Here the short walk turns right and takes the deep valley running roughly westwards back to (12). The longer walk goes left through the gate and over the remains of some of the old village buildings. The route is then waymarked round the boundary of Cottam House and after crossing the drive to the mansion we turn right, left and right again as we join one of the concrete runways of the former World War II airfield (8).

Now follows about 0.5 mile of hard surface, past the old hangar and the first runway crossing, to the next crossing at (9) where we turn right for another 1.5 miles to the minor road at (10). We go gently downhill with the unmistakeable Tatton Sykes Monument in front of us in the distance.

At the road (10) we go right for 0.5 mile to the fingerpost at (11). Here we turn off right into Cottam Well Dale. In summertime, we should be prepared to see a delightful variety of butterflies, including marbled whites, along this next stretch.

We swing left by the embayment at Elvin Lear dry valley on our right before we come to the valley junction at (12). Here the short walk joins in. Going through the gate on our left at the fence corner and walking on the left side of the fence for some 400m, we reach the junction of Cowlam Well Dale and Phillip's Slack where we were earlier in the day (3). Keeping left through the gate, we return up Cowlam Well Dale back to St Mary's Church.

Returning to the road we turn right to the signposted bridleway on our right and follow this for a short distance, through a gate, to where the track forks. Ahead to our left is the site of the medieval village, now lost beneath the ploughed field.

We take the waymarked right fork. After about 200m we come to another track division (2) and, noting the old dew pond on our right, again branch right through the gate and descend into Cowlam

Well Dale. This is a typical Woldian dry valley and twists round to the junction with Phillip's Slack at (3).

Turning left and listening for buzzards overhead, we take the wide path between the double fence line and twist along the floor of Phillip's Slack for 0.75 mile to the fingerpost and stile on our right at (4).

From here it's a short, sharp pull up the valley side to the gate at the top and from there we bear slightly left as we rise gently and follow the fieldside path. When we come to the tarred drive at (5) we turn right and continue to Cottam Grange.

Here the track turns abruptly left (6), but we continue straight ahead, using either stile or

Special Interest – Walk C

Cowlam 'at the hill-tops'
Cottam 'at the cottages'

Lost Villages

During the 14th and 15th centuries there was a widespread decline in prosperity in many parts of England and this led to the abandonment of many settlement sites. East Yorkshire is well-known for its 'lost villages' and the locations of a number of such settlements, including Cowlam and Cottam, are visited in the course of the 26 walks described in this book. Historians have identified a number of causes for the depopulation of Yorkshire villages and it will be useful to summarise these reasons.

A general worsening of the climate resulted in falling crop yields, difficulties in feeding animals and greater vulnerability to disease. In turn, this would have led to some populations declining.

During the preceding two centuries, population growth had led to new areas of marginal land being colonised. These were not always capable of sustaining permanent farming and were later abandoned. A good example would seem to be Little (or East) Givendale (Walk **Y**) where ruined houses, wasted land and the infertile, stony soils were described in reports written in the early 1400s.

Another factor was a rise in sea level which forced some populations to leave lower-lying areas along the Humber estuary and in the Vale of York.

So even before the Black Death arrived in Yorkshire in 1349, the process of village depopulation was already established but the pestilence encouraged the decline even further. It seems that few villages were completely depopulated by the Black Death; rather what appears to have happened is that villages continued on a downward spiral of decline and were then further weakened by the later plagues of the 1360s. More sinisterly, it would be far easier for landlords at a later date to force just a few tenants off the land, rather than have to deal with a bigger, thriving village.

This process of forced removal took place in the 15th and early 16th centuries. As population was declining, there was less demand for food crops but at the same time the cloth industry was expanding and so needed more wool. For an ambitious landowner keen to increase his wealth, the solution was obvious; take over your tenants' holdings and convert them from arable land to pasture and use the land for keeping bigger flocks of sheep. Much of the arable land in the old open field system was taken over in this way and then enclosed with hedges in order to contain the animals. In the case of Wharram Percy, formerly in the East Riding, it is believed that the enclosure for sheep farming completed the depopulation of the village. In 1517 the lord of the manor was reported to have put down four ploughs and allowed four houses to decay. However, Wharram's decline had started at least as early as the Black Death.

Another cause of village abandonment is the erosion by the sea of the cliffs of Holderness. This process is discussed in Walks **K** and **O**.

Cowlam had 14 houses in 1672 but had been reduced to 'the parson and two shepherds' by the 1690s. The OS map shows the location of the former settlement to the north of Church Farm. **St Mary's Church** was rebuilt in 1852 on the site of the previous structure. The Norman font, with its numerous carvings, can be seen through the window.

Cottam experienced some depopulation in the medieval period but this was not completed until the 18th century. Today it is regarded as one of the most impressive deserted village sites in Britain.

In the 14th century there had been 50 taxpayers in the village but by 1743 only one house remained. The Dean and Chapter of York owned the manor and they had given permission to their lessee to demolish most of the other houses. However, in 1841 it was recorded that there were two inhabited farmsteads containing a total of 41 people living in them. This large number is explained by the practice of boarding on the farm many of those who worked there. At Cowlam there were 44 persons living in similar conditions.

Holy Trinity Church that we see derelict today was rebuilt in 1818 and again around 1890 for the then landowner, the Rev R.H.Foord. Its Norman font was removed to Langtoft church in the mid-20th century.

Cottam Airfield was opened in 1939 with three concrete runways with the aim of being a Second World War bomber station. Yet the following year the site was abandoned because pockets of air made the landing of light aircraft hazardous. At the end of the war, it was used as a bomb dump.

ALPHABETTING IN EAST YORKSHIRE

Special Interest – Walk D

Flamborough possibly 'Flein's fortification' (or 'fortification on the promontory')

Sewerby 'Siward's farmstead'

Danes' Dyke is an extremely impressive earthwork, some 2.5 miles long, with both high banking and wide ditch. The ditch is part of a natural ravine at the south end but to the north it was artificially constructed. Its date is debatable. It was previously interpreted as a prehistoric dyke because of finds of Neolithic and Bronze Age materials. However, the construction of the dyke itself may now perhaps be more correctly placed in the Anglo-Saxon period and related to the brief encampment on Flamborough Head of King Ida in the 7th century.

Flamborough, sometimes known as the 'Capital of Little Denmark' because of its links with the Scandinavians who came around 800 AD, used to be a significant fishing port. **Ganseys** were the thick knitted jerseys worn by fishermen and each fishing settlement along the coast had its own distinctive pattern of gansey. Sometimes after shipwreck, the only means of identifying drowned bodies was by examining the ganseys.

Flamborough Castle was really a fortified manor house belonging to the Constable family who obtained permission to crenellate (erect battlements) in 1351. At one time the house included a tower, hall, parlour, chapel and court house. Today we see the remains of part of the tower.

The Old Lighthouse, the oldest in Britain, was built in 1674 as an eight-sided chalk tower but, because of the lack of assured money to buy fuel, the light was never lit. Navigation remained hazardous and between 1770 and 1806 a total of 174 ships were wrecked off Flamborough Head and the adjoining coast. **The New Lighthouse** was therefore built by Trinity House in 1806.

St Oswald's Church, Flamborough dates from around 1150 and contains a Norman font and chancel arch as well as a fine 16th century rood screen. There is also a replica of the royal pardon, 'the Strickland Pardon', granted in 1660 by King Charles II to Walter Strickland and absolving him from the charge of treason. Spare a sad smile at the the tomb of poor Sir Marmaduke Constable who is said to have swallowed a toad which ate his heart away until he eventually died.

Sewerby Hall enjoys a superb location overlooking Bridlington Bay. John Greame started building in 1714 and the Grade I listed hall is recognised as a fine example of an early Georgian mansion. The Greame family made the

house their home for over 200 years, with each generation adding to the fabric of the building. The parkland, which appears so attractive today, was laid out in the early 1800s but involved the demolition of about a dozen houses. Bridlington Corporation bought the house, gardens and parkland in 1934.

St John's Church, Sewerby is interesting. It was designed in Norman style, including zigzag carving, by G.G. Scott in 1846-1848. However, this was not the architect's preferred choice; he had to follow the whims of his employer Yarburgh Greame of Sewerby House.

In the village, Main Street, with its variety of different style old farmhouses and one-and-a-half-storey cottages, is also well worth inspection.

WALK D
Danes' Dyke

Map: Explorer 301
S.E.P.T.:   Flamborough village (227706)
Bus: 510 from Bridlington (502 on Sunday)
Longer walk (incl Sewerby):   **11.2 miles**
Longer walk (excl Sewerby):   **9.2 miles**
Shorter walk (from Flamborough village
via Beacon Hill to Danes' Dyke):   **3.0 miles**
Special interest:
         Danes' Dyke, Flamborough Head,
         Sewerby Hall

This well-known walk includes a circuit of the Flamborough Head peninsula and must class as one of Yorkshire's most spectacular. It should be obvious that the high cliffs are a potential death threat and caution must be exercised at all times. Views are at their best when the tide is out and the caves and rock platforms are most visible. As on the 'B' Walk, we are treated to a wonderful display of seabird life.

We start from the main road in the centre of Flamborough village (1) where there is bus access as well as road-side car parking.

Walking north on the road to the bend and fingerpost at (2), we turn off left on the indicated footpath. We follow field edges for a little over a mile until we come to the Headland Way path at North Cliff (3). Thistles and nettles in late July 2009 were alive with butterflies.

Turning right, we are now treated to 3.5 miles of stunning scenery with which, even in bad weather, we should be captivated. Nab, nooks and heads separate caves, coves and bays and it's not difficult to imagine the area being a smugglers' dream. Little Thornwick Bay is followed by Great Thornwick Bay and then we soon cross the deep gulley called Holmes Gut

(4). The information board tells us that this is an important resting and feeding site for migrating birds coming in from the North Sea.

After rounding North Landing Bay, the site of the old lifeboat station, we continue along the cliff-top to the cluster of buildings by the 'new' lighthouse (5). We should look at the toposcope by the beacon and the information board overlooking Selwicks Bay before carrying on along the driveway, past a fine blowhole, to the Fog Signal Station. Here we turn right to the features known as High Stacks (6).

Rounding the Headland, we now have a couple of miles on the cliff-top to South Landing, the site of the present Lifeboat Station (7). The landscape may not be so dramatic as earlier on the walk but, if the tide is out, there are still interesting views of the wave-cut rock platform below us. From South Landing the walk stays on the cliff for another mile to Danes' Dyke (8).

It's possible to turn right here and return, via the Danes' Dyke car park, to Flamborough village. However, we have the opportunity to continue to Sewerby and, if the party can be persuaded to walk an extra two miles, the

extension is well worthwhile. This is especially the case if the tide is out and we descend the steps and walk to Sewerby along the beach. If this is not possible, we follow the cliff-top path.

Assuming we have taken the beach route, we soon see the wave-cut platform and younger members of the party may just have enough energy to slow us down as they scour the rock pools. However, one unusual feature of interest to all of us is the grinding into the bedrock of multiple small circles. Examination shows that these have been made by limpets inhabiting the tidal area.

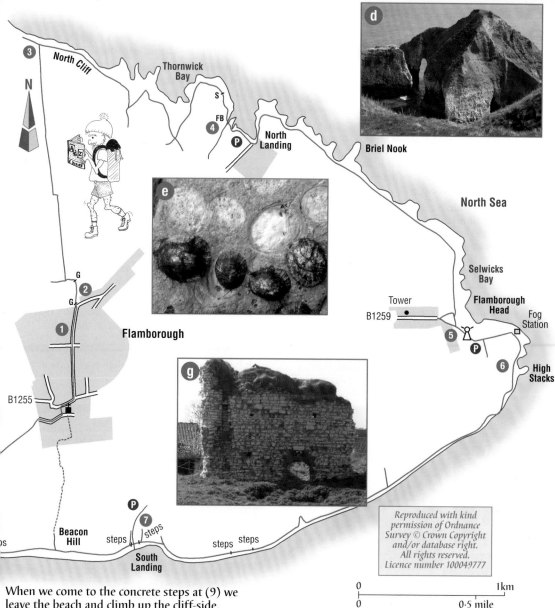

North Cliff

Thornwick Bay

N

Flamborough

Beacon Hill

B1255

B1259

Tower

North Landing

Briel Nook

North Sea

Selwicks Bay

Flamborough Head

Fog Station

High Stacks

South Landing

steps steps steps steps

0   1km
0   0·5 mile

When we come to the concrete steps at (9) we leave the beach and climb up the cliff-side. Crossing over the tarred drive, we carry straight on to the Ship Inn. If time allows, we can go left-right to visit St John's Church ahead of us; if not, a right turn will take us on the path, hard-surfaced at first, leading past Sewerby Hall and on to Danes' Dyke (10).

Just before the Dyke, the path splits into three. We take either the path on the left or the centre, black gritty route that leads down steeply into the ravine, bends left beside the stream and continues to the wooden footbridge over the water. Steps take us up the opposite side and we emerge 100m to the left of the car park.

We go straight ahead on the footpath running next to the road and take this to the bend at (11). Leaving the road, we turn right and follow field paths to the edge of Flamborough. Going down Water Lane to West Street, we cross diagonally left to Lily Lane and continue to St Oswald's Church. The path through the churchyard takes us to the main road and we bear right into the centre of the village.

Special Interest continued – Walk D

Flamborough Head

The scenery at Flamborough is exceptional and for those who used to come on School Geography field trips, today's walk offers the chance to show off their knowledge about stacks, stumps, blowholes and all the other delights of marine erosion. As always, check tide times before venturing on to the beach and remember to be careful near cliff edges.

When the tide is out, the view from the steps by the lighthouse down to **Selwicks Bay** enables us to see the large crack in the chalk rock that runs out from the cliff base into the sea. This fault has acted as a line of weakness and has made it easier for the sea to erode the Bay at his point. From the beach, a little to the right of the steps, it is easy to see the contorted mass of chalk that marks the line of the fault. The solitary pillar (or 'stack') in the Bay is known locally as 'Adam' – his mate 'Eve' on the other side of the Bay was demolished by erosion some time ago.

At the north end of the Bay lies **Molk Hole**, a small cove with its own arches and deep

undercutting at the foot of the cliffs, that gives great delight to all in the party – and not necessarily just the younger ones!

To the east of the lighthouse is **Pigeon Hole**. This is an active 'blowhole'. It has been created partly by the sea attacking a weak point in the cliff and causing a small tunnel to develop and partly by the soft boulder clay ('till') slumping down into the hollow below. When storm waves crash into the tunnel, they may send spray up the blowhole, rather like a whale sends water up its nostril.

Further round the cliff top is **High Stacks**. As this is still actually linked to the mainland by a narrow neck of till and chalk, perhaps it should not yet technically be called a 'stack'. One day, though, the sea will break through the neck and leave the stack truly separated. At low tide it is possible to use the path down the cliff-face to explore the caves and arches as well as the rock pools carved into the solid rock surface that forms the wave-cut platform.

Scattered over the platform are boulders that have fallen from the till above. One of these is composed of Shap Granite, showing that the ice which had carried it came from the Lake District. It has been dumped in an alien environment and is known as an 'erratic'.

ALPHABETTING IN EAST YORKSHIRE

Special Interest – Walk E

Everingham 'homestead of Eofor and his people'

Seaton Ross 'farm with a pool' (Ross from the family of Roos or Ross)

Holme-on-Spalding-Moor is thought to derive from 'holme', meaning an island, and a tribal group called the Spaldingas who were the offshoots or dependants of the Spalde who may have come from Lincolnshire.

Bielby 'Beli's farm'

Everingham is a former estate village acquired by one of the Constable families in the early 1500s and has long been known for its Roman Catholic associations. Yorkshire had a long history of Roman Catholic recusancy (refusal to accept the Church of England) and after the Reformation a considerable number of families remained loyal to the Roman tradition. In some places whole villages were recusant. Everingham was one of these.

Everingham Hall had been built for William H. Constable between 1757 and 1764 but it was not until after the Catholic Emancipation Act of 1829 that it became legal for Roman Catholic churches to be built. So it was only in the late 1830s that **St Mary and St Everilda's Chapel**, with its magnificent interior decorations, was constructed. In its style it bears much resemblance to Italian architecture.

Everingham, however, has a second church that is also dedicated to **St Everilda**. The other one is the Anglican foundation. It is said that there is only one other church in Britain dedicated to this saint and that is the one at Nether Poppleton in York. Little is known about Everilda but it is said that she came from Wessex in the 7th century and established a nunnery here. It has been suggested that she gave her name to 'Everingham' but Ekwall believes the origin is 'the homestead of Eofor and his people'.

Apart from the 18th century Coffee House (a former inn) and Rook House, the village was largely rebuilt in the 19th century.

Seaton Ross is known for its sundials and the village claims to have the biggest sundial in England. On Walk **E** we see the large one at Dial Cottage and a smaller one above the door of **St Edmund's Church**. However, dial-baggers may also wish to drive and see those at Dial Hall Farm (on the road to Melbourne) and at the old Wesleyan Chapel in nearby Bielby. All the sundials were the work of William Watson, a local surveyor and mapmaker, who lived at Dial Hall Farm and is buried at St Edmund's Church. Dial House Farm, on the walking route, does not possess a sundial. On William's grave is the inscription: 'At this church ... I made a Sun Dial upon the Church wall'.

Holme-on-Spalding-Moor today lies on level land below the steep slopes of Church Hill. However, it is likely that the village has migrated down the hill from the church, perhaps after the draining of the lower land, and a pre-1066 carved stone found on the hill supports this idea. In the 17th and 18th centuries an important occupation was the growing and dressing of hemp, so the village was sometimes called 'Hemp-Holme'.

All Saints Church retains its magnificent location in the Vale of York, standing on its isolated hill high above the surrounding lowlands. David Neave delights in the churchyard; 'may it never be improved' he says.

The hill owes its origin to an outcrop of Triassic Keuper marl rock standing up above the softer deposits of clay, sand and silt in the Vale of York.

Whilst in the neighbourhood, it may be possible to see **Workhouse Farm** a short distance away on the Howden Road. It was originally built about 1790 as a workhouse with separate areas for men and women. At either end were small lockups, one of which remains.

WALK E
Everingham

Maps: Explorer 291 and 294
S.E.P.: St Edmund's, Seaton Ross (781413)
Buses: 195 York-Pocklington
35 York Pullman goes to Holme

Longer walk (incl Holme):	**9.6 miles**
Medium walk (excl Holme):	**7.4 miles**
Shorter walk alternative:	**4.8 miles**
Special interest:	
Sundials	

a

THE CLOCKS

Several variations are possible for this walk. Those using public transport should start from Holme-on-Spalding-Moor but in order to cater for those doing the 4.8 mile walk the route description begins at the car park (1) at St Edmund's Church in Seaton Ross. Car drivers may wish to visit Dial Hall Farm and Bielby to see two of William Watson's sundials.

From the car park we turn left and go through the village to the crossroads at (2). We need to turn right along Carr Lane (opposite West End) but before that we should make an out-and-back visit to the Sundial Cottage some 270m further down the main road.

Proceeding along Carr Lane, we turn right after about 450m at the track junction. Then, after another 300m, we leave the track at (3) and go left beside the field edge.

A waymarked footbridge a little further on confirms our direction. From the bridge we bend diagonally right, aiming to the right of the line of trees ahead, and now follow a clear grassy path for over a mile into Everingham. At (4) we note that the p.r.o.w. and footbridge are offset on our right.

At the road (5) we turn right and continue past the parish church and the Everingham Hall driveway to the road bend at Southfield Farm (6). Going straight ahead, the short walk turns off right after 50m but the longer walk carries on.

We pass between the cultivated fields of Rolawn and then beside the open land of Everingham Carrs before we come to the fingerpost and footbridge on our left at (7). Here we leave the main track and cross two fields to arrive at two more bridges close together by the field corner. Crossing these, the p.r.o.w. then continues SSE following a drain, first on our right, then on our left, until we reach the Howdenshire (Bubwith) Rail Trail (8).

Turning left, we follow the former rail track for about 700m to the path on our right at (9). This is not shown on some OS maps and the fingerpost may have been dislodged but we leave the rail track and, following the ditch on our right, are led to the main A614 road (10).

Crossing with great care, we take the tarred drive offset to our left up to All Saints Church. It's the only hill on the walk and the panoramic views from

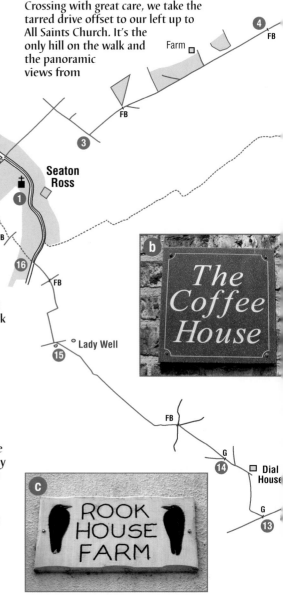

The Coffee House

b

ROOK HOUSE FARM

c

the summit amply reward our efforts. Benches outside the churchyard provide a good reason to stop for lunch.

Inspired and refreshed, we follow the path in front of us leading steeply down to the main road (11). Across to our left is Old Road and we take this as far as the signed path opposite the side road called Old Tatham.

Turning right here, we soon find that 120m beyond the houses we leave the main track and do a right-left dog-leg

(12) for 40m before the route turns NNW and follows the ditch back to the Rail Trail at (8).

Now we turn left and follow the track to the crossing by the old railway station (13). To our left is the Meadow Foods dairy products factory but we turn right and take the farm track to Dial House Farm. (The farmer prefers us to use this route rather than the awkward p.r.o.w. loop shown on the OS map.)

At the farm we bend left. When we reach the gate at (14) we have to take the grassy path to the right of the fence; not the track going through the gate to Millbrook Park stables.

Going over the River Foulness, we veer left with the hedge on our right and then bend right at the end of the hedge. The path gets wider as it crosses farmland and we note the 'elephant grass' (miscanthus) being grown as a biofuel for Drax power station. Ahead of us, hidden in bushes, is the site of Lady Well, one of numerous wells in the country dedicated to the Virgin Mary.

The track swings left and right, then bends left again and here the p.r.o.w. has been diverted to go around the field edge (15). We leave the track and bear right with the hedge on our left. Further waymarks direct us right, then left to the gap in the hedge.

From here there are two more small fields to cross before we reach the Black Horse pub in Seaton Ross (16). A right turn along the road takes us back to our start.

Everingham

Hall

Everingham Park

Southfield Farm

N

Everingham Carrs

FB

FB
FB

Rail Trail

A614

Church Hill

Holme-on-Spalding-Moor

0   1km
0   0·5 mile

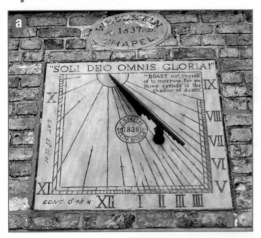

Special Interest – Walk F

Fridaythorpe 'Fridag's village'
(The village information board suggests other possible spellings, e.g., 'Frigedaeg's village'.)

Church Architecture

English Parish Churches are places of Christian worship and not museums. However, every church is a priceless record of the history of a local community and the churches we visit in this book allow us to reflect on some of those spiritual, social and economic stories.

Norman churches, with their square towers and rounded arches, had only small windows which left the church interiors dark and gave worshippers a feeling of awe and mystery.

This changed with the introduction of '**Gothic**' architecture which is the general name given to the variety of styles that characterised English church building from about 1190 to around 1530. Gothic building styles are characterised by slender spires, pointed arches and large windows through which the light of God could shine.

During the 1600s and 1700s Classical and Renaissance styles became fashionable and few churches were built in the Gothic style.

Then in the 19th century the '**Gothic Revival**' began with an astonishing expansion of church building in which Victorian architects developed their own rich interpretations of the old medieval Gothic styles. East Yorkshire was fortunate to have the Sykes family from Sledmere as patrons for a remarkable number of church building programmes.

The Sykes Churches Trail is an itinerary through East Yorkshire to some of the region's most fascinating churches. The buildings on the route were all built, rebuilt or restored by Sir Tatton Sykes I (1772-1863) and his son Sir Tatton Sykes II (1826-1913). It was Tatton Sykes I who employed J.L. Pearson as architect and Tatton Sykes II who used G.E. Street and Temple Moore as designers.

Between 1866 and 1913 Tatton Sykes II financed the work on a total of 17 rural churches in the region. St Mary's Church, Cowlam, is on the Sykes Trail and was visited on Walk **C** while St Mary's Church on the present Walk **F** was also restored by him. Others churches on the Sykes Trail can be seen on Walks **N**, **W** and **Y**.

St Mary's Church, Fridaythorpe is a Norman foundation with, according to Pevsner & Neave, an 'utterly barbaric south doorway'. Others, of course, may think the variety of carvings charmingly attractive. On one of the piers in the north arcade there is a cryptic inscription that

reads: 'This 713 found hear' – see who in your party can devise the most plausible explanation!

The Sykes restoration took place in 1902-03. The north aisle, long demolished, was rebuilt and also the south porch and vestry.

'The Battle of Fimber', July 1826. During a severe drought, the residents of Fimber allowed Fridaythorpe villagers to use the water supply from their two meres. But then the Fimberians withheld their goodwill gesture. Outraged, the Fridaythorpers marched with their cattle to Fimber and gave battle. The gallant Fimberians withstood the onslaught and repulsed the invaders. That same evening the drought ended and heavy rain fell on the erstwhile combatants.

The 'Roman' Gateposts that can be seen west of Fridaythorpe were the inspiration of Newark Andrews who had them erected in the 1970s. The County Council had decreed that all gateways opening on to roadways had to be marked in some way. Newark decided to make an eccentric statement and had some 40 bollards erected around his property, the former Wold Farm. Using an old copper cylinder as a mould, he poured in concrete to produce the gateposts, each with its special lettering. Many of the inscriptions are supposedly in Latin, though translations are sometimes puzzling!

WALK F
Fridaythorpe

Map: Explorer 294
S.E.P.:   St Mary's Church, F'thorpe (875592)
Bus: 135 from Driffield
Longer walk (via Wayrham):   **9.3 miles**
Medium walk (via Pluckham):   **8.0 miles**
Shorter walk (via Wold House Farm): **5.4 miles**
Special interest:
          Sykes Churches Trail

Starting from St Mary's Church in Fridaythorpe (1), we walk to the A166, turn right in the direction of York, branch off left from the main road at the Wolds Way indicator and go down Huggate Lane.

The tarmac soon gives way to mud and at the track crossing (2) we stay on the Wolds Way as we are led down, through the gate, into Holm Dale. This is the first of the day's typical Woldian dry valleys.

After staying left of the fence at (3), we soon reach Horse Dale valley. We turn right through the gate in front of us (still following the Wolds Way) but quickly leave the valley floor on the path sloping gently up on our left.

Near the top of the valley side (4), we use open access concessions and, instead of continuing on the Wolds Way, bear right and follow the contour along what the

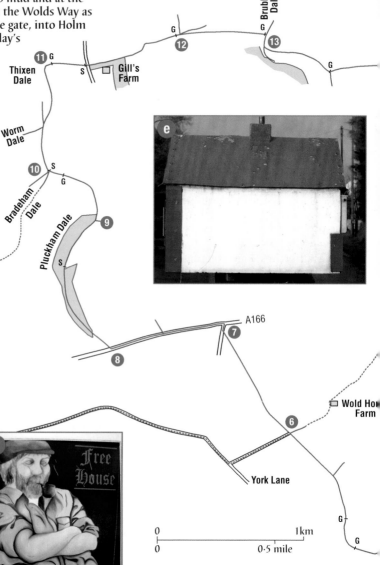

0 ——————————— 1km
0 ——————————— 0·5 mile

OS map shows as prehistoric linear earthworks. Views down to the right are especially memorable.

Carrying on to (5), we notice a waymarked gate up to our left and then soon swing down the slope to go through the gate at the bottom. Some 50m after this, we bend right and take the tributary dry valley branching up to our right. After another gate, we stay by the field edge and come to the track crossing at (6)*.

From here the shorter walk turns right, goes through Wold House Farm and back to Fridaythorpe. The Pluckham Dale route continues straight on beside the hedge but the longer Wayrham Picnic itinerary goes left.

We emerge on a side road, go 30m right and turn left (7) on to the A166. Using the wide grassy verge, we continue along the road and, ignoring the driveway to Pluckham Farm, carry on to the fingerpost at (8). Here we turn right.

Following the fieldside at first, we need to be careful not to miss the entry into the trees of Pluckham Plantation, after which we walk through the wood down Pluckham Dale. The path may be a little overgrown in summer but the route stays on the floor of the valley and we eventually leave the trees at a

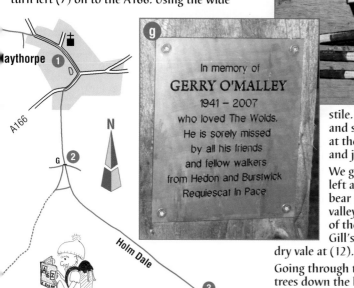

In memory of
GERRY O'MALLEY
1941 – 2007
who loved The Wolds.
He is sorely missed
by all his friends
and fellow walkers
from Hedon and Burstwick
Requiescat In Pace

stile. We continue to the fence corner and swing left at (9), bend left again at the valley Y-fork, go through a gate and join Bradeham Dale (10).

We go right, pass Worm Dale to our left and at the Wolds Way fingerpost bear right up the side of Thixen Dale valley. The path turns right at the top of the slope (11) and continues past Gill's Farm to the head of yet another dry vale at (12).

Going through the gate, we follow the line of old trees down the bottom of the valley and come to Brubber Dale. We turn right alongside the fence until we see the wide grassy track of the Wolds Way rising up the other side of the valley at (13). Crossing over, we follow this route to the gate at the top of the slope. Here we bear left and it's an easy stroll back into Fridaythorpe.

*Note: it is possible to avoid walking along the A166 if we turn left at (6) and walk to York Lane. A right turn on this minor road will lead us to the Wayrham picnic site. We can then cross the A166 and follow Wayrham Dale and Bradeham Dale to the path junction at (10). However, this latter section will be repeated, in the reverse direction, on the **P** Walk.

WALK G
Gypsey Race

Map: Explorer 301
S.E.P.:   St Cuthbert's, Burton Fleming
          (083723)
Bus: 124 from Driffield three days a week
Longer walk (incl Monument):   **11.5 miles**
Longer walk (excl Monument):   **10.4 miles**
Shorter walk alternative: **7.0 miles**
Special interest:
          Gypsey Race, Meteorite Site

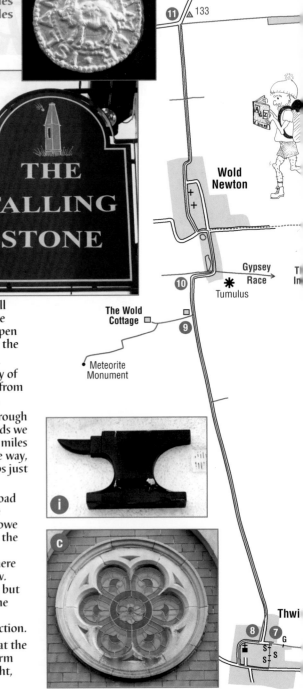

Turning right, we make our way into Thwing on the grassy track.

Passing through the first farmyard, we carry on to the signposted path 60m further on (7). We turn left here, cross a couple of small fields and go along a narrow path to Main Street.

This walk links three attractive villages each with its own church and its own pub. Although over half of the route is on tarmac, the roads are quiet and for long stretches without hedges, so there are good views in all directions across the Wolds. The first time we investigated this route we saw deer on the open farmland and watched barn owls hunting in the early evening.

It is possible to commence the walk from any of the three villages but this description starts from St Cuthbert's Church in Burton Fleming (1).

After looking in the church, we walk SSW through the village down Front Street. At the crossroads we turn right along Wold Newton Road for 1.25 miles to the sharp right turn at (2). For part of the way, we will have noticed the Gypsey Race, perhaps just a dry ditch, next to the road on our right.

At (2) the short walk turns right along the road but the longer route carries on ahead on the tarred farm drive. Soon we pass the Willy Howe tumulus on our left. Then when we come to the short path leading off right to the farm slurrystore tank, we continue for 30m and here turn left off the tarmac drive (3). The p.r.o.w. shown on the OS map cuts across two fields but the farmer requests that we walk between the two different crops (there's no actual field boundary) at about 10.00/11.00 o'clock direction.

At the transverse hedge (4) we go right and at the next hedge (5) we turn left on to a chalky farm trail. When we reach Thwing Road we go right, bend left and come to the fingerpost at (6).

A right turn leads us over the staggered crossroads and we soon turn right at Church Lane and walk up to All Saints Church. This is another treasure that well deserves our attention before we leave by the gate on the north side of the churchyard.

We turn right and go to the road indicator post (8), by Pear Tree Farm, that directs us left towards Wold Newton. Following this direction, we continue to the third of the villages on this walk.

As we approach Wold Newton, we see fine views of the broad valley of the Gypsey Race. We note how the village and its neighbour to our left, Foxholes, both occupy south-facing slopes in order to catch maximum sunshine. Ahead of us to our right lie The Ings, the seasonally flooded land that nearly made this walk the 'I' Walk.

Before the village, we pass the drive to The Wold Cottage (9). The owners allow us on to their land to see The Meteorite Monument but please phone in advance (01262 470696) and remember that this generous concession in no way confers any legal right of public access.

At the edge of Wold Newton (10), the road turns sharp right along the Gypsey Race. Soon we bend left into the village and come to the crossroads and Wold Newton's village pond. Two minor roads lead north from here; we take the one on the left (Front Street) signed to the ancient church. Here at All Saints, we find another fascinating reminder of the Christian heritage of East Yorkshire.

N

Windmill
Country Park

Gypsey Race

②

✳ Willy Howe

③

Willy Howe □
Farm

⑤   ④

Burton
Fleming   ①

Gypsey Race

⑫

⑬

FREE HOUSE

BURTON
ARMS

B&B ACCOMMODATION

Leaving the church, photo-clue treasure hunters need to be alert as we carry on up the road. At the end of the houses, we twist right and left as we leave the village and then continue up the north side of the wide Great Wold Valley.

Just before the trig point (11), there is a four-way road-track junction. We turn sharp right and take the wide track known as North Cotes Road that leads to the road at (13). It is straight except for a right-left kink at (12).

Joining the road at (13) we go right for about 100m to the road crossing and then carry on straight ahead and, passing the Windmill Country Park, arrive back in Burton Fleming.

0   1km
0   0·5 mile

Special Interest – Walk G

Burton Fleming 'fortified homestead of the Flemings' (the family that held Burton in the 12th century)

Thwing uncertain; perhaps 'the strip of land'

Wold Newton 'new farm' on the Wolds. In Old English 'weald' meant forest land; later it came to mean 'any waste land in lofty country'

Fordon 'in front of the hill'

'Gypsies' are streams that only flow from time to time. There are a number in the Wolds region but the only one of significance is **The Gypsey Race**. This is the name of the stream that flows across the northern Wolds from a spring near Duggleby, through the Great Wold Valley, to the North Sea at Bridlington. We have already seen how on the Wolds there are scores of valleys that are now dry because water easily soaks down into the permeable chalk rock below. The presence of water at the ground surface in the Gypsey Race,

therefore, has made the stream extremely important for thousands of years.

Important Neolithic sites occur along the line of the Great Wold Valley at Duggleby Howe, Willy Howe and Rudston and it seems reasonable to assume that the presence of nearby water was a major factor in their establishment.

Centuries after, Anglian settlements such as the Luttons and Wold Newton, as well as later Scandinavian villages like Duggleby and Weaverthorpe, were attracted by the springs along the course of the Gypsey Race.

Although we may see little water in the stream when we visit, the naming of 'Ings' on the map shows that, at times, the river can flood and records tell us that in 1327 nine houses and their lands were 'wasted' by flooding. To counter the stream's erratic flow, ponds were commonly created to conserve water. We meet the Gypsey Race again on Walks **X** and **Z**.

Burton Fleming is known as the village where Queen Henrietta Maria spent a night in 1643 on

Gypsey Race

Willy Howe

American science fiction writer Philip Jose Farmer used the incident to create an imaginative tale. People who were passing by at the time suffered genetic mutation and their altered genes led to extraordinary developments in their descendants. These included Tarzan, Sherlock Holmes and James Bond. The extended family of superheroes and villains is now known as the 'Wold Newton Family'.

The meteorite has also been commemorated by the production of Falling Stone Bitter beer. This is one of a number of locally brewed beers produced by the Wold Top Brewery on the Burton Fleming road.

All Saints Church, like its namesake at Thwing, has a Norman south doorway and chancel arch and a Norman drum-shaped font.

her journey from Bridlington to York taking arms and reinforcements for the Royalist cause during the English Civil War.

St Cuthbert's Church shows evidence of much repair work and, like other churches in the region, contains a mixture of stone, cobble and brick. It looks charming to us but church officers would never get permission to build like that today!

A large Late Neolithic henge lies just SE of the village and to the SW is an extensive linear settlement dated to the Romano-British period.

Willy Howe lies about a mile to the east of the village and is a giant round barrow some 40m across. When excavated, a large central grave pit was uncovered but without corpses or grave goods. It is thought to be of Late Neolithic date.

Fordon hamlet is part of the civil parish of Wold Newton. **St James' Church** merits a visit (perhaps by car at the end of the walk) because of its peaceful seclusion. Norman stonework is found but the 1768 date above the door probably refers to the insertion of the pointed windows in the south and west walls.

Thwing was the birthplace of St John of Bridlington (1320-1379), the last English saint to be canonised before the Reformation.

All Saints Church, Thwing was restored in 1898-1901 but some of the older parts, such as the south doorway and chancel arch dating from about 1150, were retained.

Thomas Lamplugh, who became Archbishop of York in 1688, was born at nearby Octon, in Thwing parish. Lamplugh House conference centre in Thwing is named after him.

In 2003 a person using a metal detector at Thwing found a gold-covered Bronze Age ring dating from around 1150-750 BC.

Wold Newton holds an important place in our understanding of extraterrestrial activity because it was here on 13th December 1795 that a meteorite hit the earth. The origin of the smouldering lump of rock caused great scientific speculation but it was eventually decided that this UFO was, indeed, made of a material unlike anything else on earth. A brick obelisk marks the location of the impact and the landowner usually gives permission to view the monument.

Meteorite Monument

WALK H
Huggate

Map: Explorer 294
S.E.P.: St Mary's Church, Huggate (882555)
Bus: No bus service
Longer walk distance: **9.1 miles**
Shorter walk alternative: **5.0 miles**
Special interest:
      Huggate Dykes

This walk can be divided into two loops centred on Huggate village. Navigation is easy and sections of the route follow the waymarked Wolds Way, Minster Way and Chalkland Way.

Starting from St Mary's Church, Huggate (1) we turn right on to the main street and go north out of the village. Joining a short stretch of the Wolds Way, we continue along the road to the Chalkland Way fingerpost (2).

This directs us right into Cow Dale and we continue along the floor of this dry valley to the gate at the path T-junction at (3). Turning right through the gate, we now twist along two more dry valleys, Oxlands Dale and Shortlands Dale, to the gate at (4).

The path has been redirected to the left of the trees, so we walk with the copse on our right, turn right at the farm track and carry on to the minor road at (5)

At this point we turn right and continue along the road, past the Tibthorpe turn-off (6), to the junction at (7). A left turn takes us some 500m to the bridleway crossing at (8). Now we turn right and follow a section of the Minster Way.

It's a flat, field edge path with good views to our left as we make our way to Mill Lane (9). On the way we see scores of cloches for growing soft fruit. Fancy – strawberries on top of the Wolds – what's

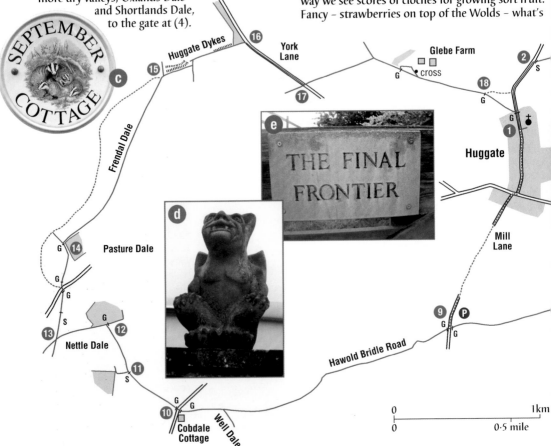

     ALPHABETTING IN EAST YORKSHIRE

Geography coming to! At Mill Lane the short walk turns right and returns to Huggate.

The longer walk crosses the road and goes straight ahead along the wide track known as Hawold Bridle Road. We stay level as we make our way to the head of Well Dale dry valley and on to Cobdale Cottage on Cobdale Lane (10). Crossing over, we continue to the head of Nettle Dale dry valley (11).

We can now make use of Open Access arrangements on to Millington Pastures. About 100m before the p.r.o.w. fingerpost we can see ahead of us, we cross the stile on our right and now follow the fence line along to Jessop's Plantation (12). (This short-cut saves us the rather

tedious trek along Nettle Dale and then back up the steep northern side of the valley.) Here we join the Wolds Way.

We turn left and the path above Nettle Dale descends gently to the junction at (13). A right turn takes us up, over and down the spur to the road in Pasture Dale. Crossing to the gate offset slightly to our left, we come to Frendal Dale.

Rather than using the p.r.o.w. along the valley floor, we may prefer to bear right to the stile that leads us up the steep convex slope to a small fenced plantation (14). We turn left along the fence as far as the gate on our right, go through the gate and follow the fence round the top side of Frendal Dale.

It's not long before we see that we are tracing the line of a linear earthwork and then where the fence bends right (15) we count four parallel ditches and embankments. These are the remains of the Huggate Dykes and we can spend a few minutes wondering why on earth prehistoric man bothered to construct such impressive monuments.

We swing right, following the fence, to the stile at the far end of the dykes and then continue on the farm track to York Lane (16).

A right turn brings us to the Wolds Way crossing (17) where we go left on the tarred drive towards Glebe Farm. We bend right after 500m and then, using the waymarked path forking right by the first buildings, we are led round the edge of the farmstead to join the tarred road a little further on. If we look back left towards the farm, we can see the ancient cross socket on the left of the driveway.

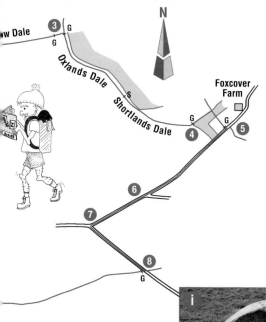

Carrying on down the slope, we come back into Huggate either by turning right at the road T-junction or by using the p.r.o.w. (18) to cut off the road corner. Before we leave the village, treasure hunters should make a point of finding the covered well.

VILLAGE WELL
339 ft DEEP

Special Interest – Walk H

Huggate possibly 'the road to the mounds' (the tumuli on Huggate Wold)

Huggate is the highest village on the Wolds and possesses one of the deepest wells (111m or 365') in England.

St Mary's Church has a Norman nave, aisles and chancel arch. Rather puzzling are the two small windows above the arch because they are higher than the original roof line as marked against the tower. The tower dates from the early 14th century.

Strawberries on the Wolds are a fascinating example of how farming practices are subject to change. The Wolds are usually thought of as sheep rearing pastures or as arable farmland. Nevertheless, Chris Hoggard of Newby Farm, Huggate has been operating a commercial strawberry farm since 1991, supplying large supermarket chains and small local farm shops with fresh Wolds strawberries. At first this sounds surprising because the Wolds are relatively high and so exposed to possible cool weather and therefore not a preferred natural location for growing soft fruit. However, the crop is protected by polythene tunnels that act like giant cloches. Members of The National Strawberry Breeding Club have access to a wide range of different types of strawberry. Among the varieties grown at Huggate are Christine, Sonata, Elsanta, Florence and Marshmallow.

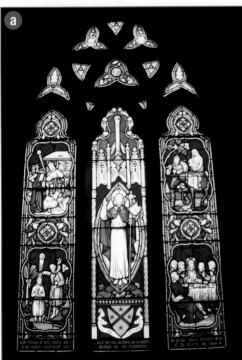

They fruit at different times of the summer and so stagger the season's harvest; their names certainly sound prettier than some of the apple varieties we see on Walk **J**!

Prehistoric Dykes

Long linear embankments (also known as dykes or entrenchments or linears) are an important feature of the Wolds landscape. They are mostly made up of at least two parallel ditches and bankings but the Huggate Dykes contain six embankments. They have largely been ploughed out but the remnant at Huggate is probably the best example left on the Wolds.

It is not certain why the dykes were built but a common theory is that they acted as prehistoric land boundaries. Whether they also had a defensive role is not clear. From excavations it is known that they were laid out at different times between about 1000 BC and 1000 AD. Late Bronze Age pottery remains unearthed at Thwing were discovered at the bottom of the ditches, suggesting an actual date for their construction. Later the ditches became partly filled in and Roman pottery was found in the upper levels of the soil.

However, the digging of ditched boundaries was not limited to only one period of history and in other places it has been confirmed that some were dug in the Iron Age (one at Cowlam dates from after 300 BC) or in the Roman period itself.

It has been observed that the biggest dyke systems are found stretched across the narrow necks of land separating the heads of adjacent dry valleys. This is particularly the case with the Huggate Dykes which run between Horse Dale and Tun Dale. In many cases the entrenchments made use of earlier barrows as markers to determine their lines of direction. The Great Wold Dyke is one example. Single ditches without banks are found only along the upper slopes of minor dry valleys.

Chris Fenton-Thomas summarises the importance of the dykes by suggesting that before the late Bronze Age (i.e., before about 1000 BC) the landscape had been dotted with burial tumuli and significant natural features such as meres and isolated trees. These would have been reached by a network of trackways. As the countryside became more enclosed with the building of the dykes at the end of the Bronze Age, these trackways could be used as demarcation boundaries. The Sledmere Green Lane (Walk **W**) is a good example.

Special Interest – Walk 1

Low Catton Ings and Lower Derwent Valley National Nature Reserve

The word 'Ings' does not appear in Chambers Dictionary but it is an old Norse word meaning 'winter-flooded grassland'. Landholding in the Lower Derwent Valley NNR is complicated but within the NNR there are four SSSIs, one of which is **Newton Mask**. The adjacent **Low Catton Ings** is managed by Carstairs Countryside Trust but is subject to the same international conservation directives.

English Nature describes the Lower Derwent Valley as one of the last great areas of winter-flooded grassland in England and as such it is of international importance. The landscape has remained largely unchanged for over a thousand years.

For centuries The Ings have supported local communities in their haymaking, wildfowling, grazing, fishing and basket-making activities.

Good quality hay was important as winter feed for livestock and when the hay had been carted away, the fields were grazed by cattle or sheep until the end of autumn. 'Ings-masters' may well have delegated the oversight of the animals to other workers at this time. Snowden Slights made his living here in the early 20th century, shooting wildfowl in winter and acting as fisherman and basket weaver in the summer.

Newton Mask is a single large meadow. Different parts of the field have different flooding patterns, depending on how far they are from the River Derwent, and this means that they have different types of plant species. To the uninitiated, some of the names make wonderful reading: fairy flax, adder's-tongue fern and yellow rattle pignut all grow on the area further away from the river.

There is a regular seasonal cycle of life on the Ings of the Lower Derwent Valley. In spring, resident moorhen, lapwing and curlew start breeding, along with mallard, teal, shoveler and gadwall. The distinctive 'drumming' of snipe can be heard at twilight or early morning. At the same season, huge flocks of wildfowl, swans and wading birds leave and go to their breeding grounds in the Arctic tundra. Summer time sees the arrival of migrants such as warblers, wheatears and blackcaps and by the beginning of autumn we can expect to see hundreds of golden plover around the edge of the Ings. Winter will find thousands of wigeon and teal coming back from northern Europe to feed in the grass at the edge of flooded areas. 'Whooping' whooper, and 'bugling' Bewick's swans, together with raucous geese, add to the variety of sounds heard across the floodplain.

Otters are known to fish the River Derwent.

Wilberfoss used to have a Benedictine nunnery, founded about 1150. This was located north of **St John the Baptist's Church** which has remnants of Norman architecture.

In recent years the village has received attention because of its association with the family of William Wilberforce, the great anti-slavery campaigner. At least 20 generations of the family, although not William Wilberforce himself, have lived here. William Hague records how the family could trace its ancestral line with certainty to the village of Wilberfoss in the time of Henry II (1154-89).

All Saints Church, Low Catton still retains some of its Norman origins, such as the north transept. The east window is said to be the best example of Victorian stained glass in the East Riding.

Kexby Bridge A bridge was built here in the late 1420s by Nicholas Blackburn. The present structure, rebuilt in 1650 and repaired in 1778, probably includes material from the medieval bridge. The arms of the Ughtred family can be seen on a stone at the west side.

Stamford Bridge has an important place in British history. It was here in 1066 that King Harold Godwinson of England defeated his brother Tostig and Harald Hardrader of Norway after Hardrader had earlier crushed an English army at the Battle of Fulford. So the Scandinavian threat was over but the English were immediately faced with another battle, this time with William the Conqueror at the other end of the country. The result of that encounter was entirely different for Harold.

Dominating the centre of Stamford Bridge is the **watermill**. The main block was built in the 19th century when the mill had two waterwheels. It ceased working in 1964.

Adjacent to the **bridge** erected in 1727 over the River Derwent is a **lock** that had been built a few years earlier to make the river navigable up to Malton.

The town used to have a chapel with a hermit in 1348. Modern worshippers can use either the **Methodist Chapel** (1828) or **St John the Baptist** Anglican Church (1868).

WALK I
The Ings

Map: Explorer 294
S.E.P.: Wilberfoss Church (732510)
or Stamford Bridge car park (711555)
Bus: X46 York-Hull
Longer walk (incl the Cattons): **9.2 miles**
Shorter walk (excl the Cattons): **7.7 miles**
Extension (incl Stamford Bridge): **11.1 miles**
Special interest:
Low Catton Ings and Lower Derwent
Valley NNR, Stamford Bridge

Stamford Bridge 'stone-paved ford' (later replaced by a bridge)

High/Low Catton 'Catta's farm'

Kexby either 'Kek's farm' or 'farmstead overgrown with kex plants'

Wilberfoss 'Wilburg's ditch'

Newton upon Derwent 'new farmstead' on Derwent

This is another walk of two loops. The northern loop includes a fair amount of road but allows us to visit Stamford Bridge and the site of the 1066 Battle. The southern loop includes a section of the Jorvic Way.

Starting at St John the Baptist's Church (1) we walk south through the village to the A1079 road, cross carefully and take the signposted p.r.o.w. offset to our left.

Waymarked gates and stiles direct us across half a dozen fields and through the hedge at (2) and we continue, with Cobb Flatts Farm on our right, to the telecommunications tower at the next field boundary. Going through the cupressus hedge, we follow the ditch and hedge on our right for a short way before crossing to the right-hand side of the watercourse. The path, between two fields, is now clear to Carr Lane at (3).

We turn right and follow the road, which changes name to Bull Balk, to the T-junction at (4), turn right, then first left, on to Jackson Lane and come to the edge of Newton upon Derwent.

Turning right into Mask Lane, we continue for about a mile along what soon becomes a rough track, to the gate at (5). Here we have access to the Newton Mask and Low Catton Ings and the alphabetical reason for this walk.

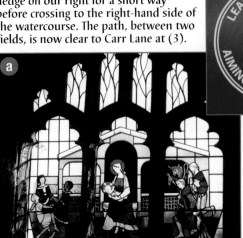

We cross the grass to the side of the River Derwent and are now in the Lower Derwent Valley National Nature Reserve. From here the route is delightful as we bear right and take the riverside path to Kexby Bridge (6).

As we go under the arch of the old bridge, we bend right and come up to the old road. If we turn back to our right, we can investigate the inscriptions on the bridge more fully, but the main route goes on to the A1079.

Again crossing with care, we use the pavement as we walk in the Wilberfoss direction, past Kexby House, to the bridleway turn at (7). Leaving the road, we take the farm track to the road corner at Town End Farm (8). At this point the short walk turns right along Broad Lane to the private drive at (11).

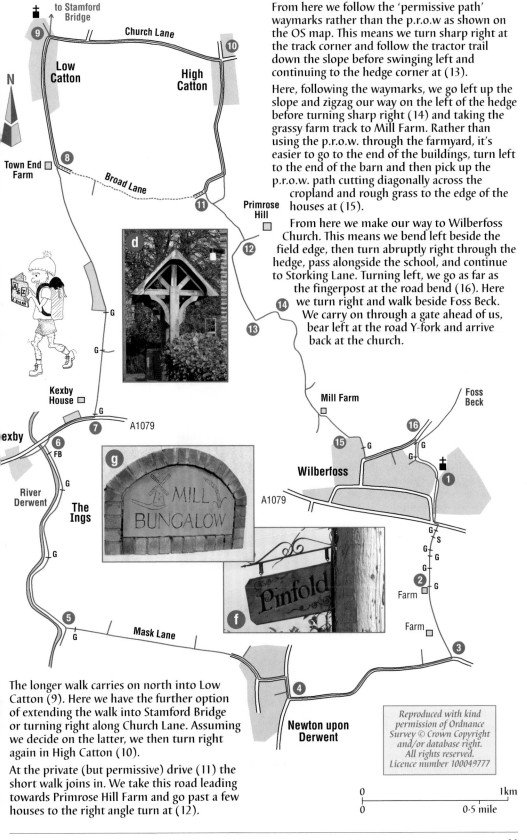

N

to Stamford Bridge

Church Lane

Low Catton

High Catton

Town End Farm

Broad Lane

Primrose Hill

d

G

G

Kexby House

G

exby

A1079

FB

River Derwent

The Ings

G

g

MILL BUNGALOW

G

Mask Lane

f

Pinfold

Mill Farm

Foss Beck

Wilberfoss

A1079

G **G**

G **S**

G **G**

G

Farm

G

Farm

Newton upon Derwent

From here we follow the 'permissive path' waymarks rather than the p.r.o.w as shown on the OS map. This means we turn sharp right at the track corner and follow the tractor trail down the slope before swinging left and continuing to the hedge corner at (13).

Here, following the waymarks, we go left up the slope and zigzag our way on the left of the hedge before turning sharp right (14) and taking the grassy farm track to Mill Farm. Rather than using the p.r.o.w. through the farmyard, it's easier to go to the end of the buildings, turn left to the end of the barn and then pick up the p.r.o.w. path cutting diagonally across the cropland and rough grass to the edge of the houses at (15).

From here we make our way to Wilberfoss Church. This means we bend left beside the field edge, then turn abruptly right through the hedge, pass alongside the school, and continue to Storking Lane. Turning left, we go as far as the fingerpost at the road bend (16). Here we turn right and walk beside Foss Beck. We carry on through a gate ahead of us, bear left at the road Y-fork and arrive back at the church.

The longer walk carries on north into Low Catton (9). Here we have the further option of extending the walk into Stamford Bridge or turning right along Church Lane. Assuming we decide on the latter, we then turn right again in High Catton (10).

At the private (but permissive) drive (11) the short walk joins in. We take this road leading towards Primrose Hill Farm and go past a few houses to the right angle turn at (12).

0 _____ 1km

0 _____ 0·5 mile

WALK J
Jillywood Lane

Map: Explorer 293
S.E.P.:   All Hallows, Walkington (998368)
Bus: 180 Beverley-Hessle
Longer walk distance: **11.8 miles**
Shorter walk (based on Bentley):   **4.5 miles**
Special interest:
           Jillywood Lane, Beverley Westwood,
           Millennium Orchard, Risby Park

Parking at All Hallows Church (1) we walk back and turn right down Kirk Lane, right on the B1230 through Walkington village, right up All Hallows Road and right at Ferguson Road to join the Beverley 20 footpath. Here we turn left along the grit path and field edge to the road at (2).

Going right, we walk for about 500m before turning off left on the track known as Moor Lane (3). This is a pleasant, twisting track that takes us through a small copse and when we leave the trees we turn sharp left (4). Waymarks guide us back to the B1230 road (5).

We cross the road, turn right to pass above the A1079 and immediately go left on the signed Beverley 20 path. Walking parallel to the A1079, we follow a wide track to the small gate at (6). Here we turn off right.

When we come to the gate at the edge of the Westwood (7), we go ahead for 100m and then swing right, following the fairway, up over the hummocks of the golf course to head straight for Black Mill on the skyline.

From Black Mill we go south over the grass to another old mill that now forms the golf clubhouse – the cluster of cars gives us our direction. Crossing the B1230 again and continuing to the left of the former mill, we turn left at the boundary fence and walk to the gate and path at (8). Now we turn right and leave the Westwood.

After about 200m we go through the kissing gate on our left. We soon have to turn right and an attractive tree-lined track takes us round the side of the large chalk quarry on our right. When we reach the recreation area in front of us we turn left and walk, going between a few houses, to the A164.

We turn right, cross the road and, ignoring the first tarred path on our left, go for a little over 350m to the hard-surfaced path at (9). Turning left, we come to a suburban road but cross straight over on to Shepherd Lane. We follow this

quiet road to Old Hall Farm (10). Here we pause at the Millennium Orchard.

From the Orchard, we turn right along the edge of the grass, cross the duckboarded ditch and join the p.r.o.w. at (11). A right turn on this gravel track takes us past Model Farm. Soon we are directed 90° left and, following the hedge, we carry on and cross the bridge over the A1079 road (12).

The p.r.o.w. splits; we take the tarred lane bearing left and leading to Poplar Farm. Here the path is waymarked around the buildings and, after an initial right turn, we go left and right before following the hedge on our right. This brings us to the path junction by a small pond at (13). We turn right, staying on the Beverley Beaver Trail.

For the next section of the walk, we continue beside a meandering ditch. The OS map labels the two fields on our left as 'Jillywoods' but there is no sign of any trees apart from those in the hedgerows.

We pass through a wide gap at the first hedge and then after the second (14), the path is tree-lined on both sides. This is Jillywood Lane.

At the tarred cycle track we turn right to the A164 road. **We cross this busy main road with extreme care.** On the opposite side we continue on the minor road in front of us but at the sharp right bend (15) we go straight on in the direction of Risby Park Fisheries.

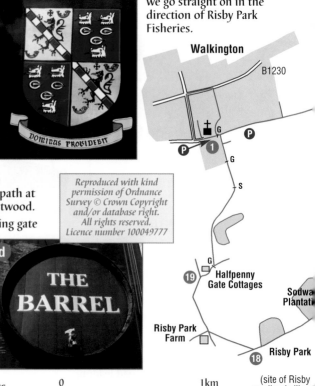

DOMINUS PROVIDEBIT

THE BARREL

Walkington

B1230

Halfpenny Gate Cottages

Sodwa Plantati

Risby Park Farm

Risby Park

(site of Risby medieval village

0   1km
0   0·5 mile

Just after the road bends right, then left, we turn off right (16) on the Beaver Trail and, following waymarks along the edge of Fishpond Wood, we are led round to the Walkington road at (17). We go left for about 50m and turn off left on the signed footpath.

The path follows the edges of fields over Risby Park and then down the slope to the path junction at (18). Here we fork right over the farm land and up to Risby Park Farm.

At the farm we bear right and continue to Halfpenny Gate

Cottages (19). Here the track divides into two. We again turn right, staying on the Beverley 20 route, but after 200m go through the gate in the hedge on our left.

Walking beside the wood on our right, the grassy path soon bends right and we aim for the stile in the far corner of the field. From here, the track leads us back to Walkington and All Hallows Church.

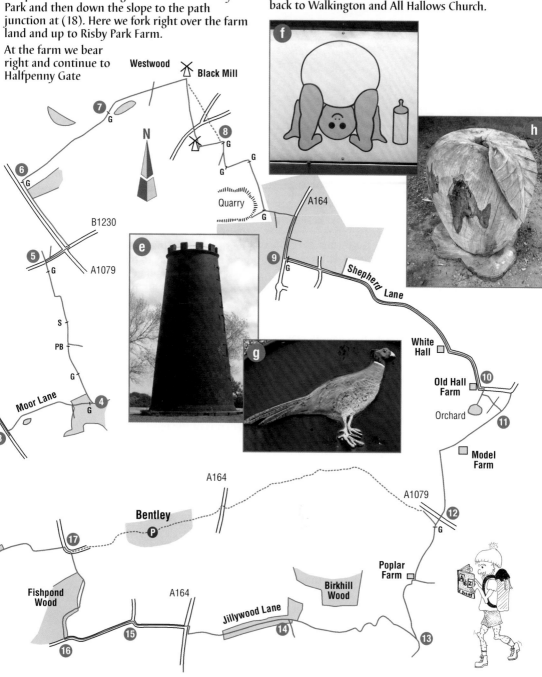

Special Interest – Walk J

Walkington 'Walca's farm'
Beverley probably 'beaver stream or lake'
Risby probably 'farm near the clearing'
Bentley 'clearing overgrown with coarse grass'
Skidby probably 'Skyti's farm'

Jillywood Lane

The ancient parish of Skidby included a small piece of land separated from the village and located several miles away to the east beside the River Hull. This detached area was one of meadows and common carr land which was important for the grazing of animals. To reach this territory, the people of Skidby had to cross land belonging to the Lord of Bentley Manor and, from at least the early 1500s, they had to make an annual payment for this privilege.

The route taken is thought to have gone north from Skidby along the track shown on the OS map as Oldgate. It then turned east, and north, along the Bentley parish boundary. Still following the boundary, it turned east again on what is now called Jillywood Lane. This is the section followed on Walk J and also the route used by the Beverley Beaver Running Trail.

Unfortunately this ancient track is today blocked near Poplar Farm but it continues further to the east as Skidby Carr Lane.

But why 'Jillywood'? In old records of 1269 the Jillywoods are called 'Suthwode' (woods belonging to the Hospital of St Giles in Beverley) and 'Jilly' seems to have replaced 'Gilly' (for Giles). On the present OS map, 'Jillywoods' is written over two arable fields but on the 1850 OS map one of these fields was still wooded and the trees continued up to Birkhill Wood. (Confusingly, local people today sometimes call these woods the Jillywoods!)

All Hallows Church, Walkington has interior arches dating from about 1200 as well as medieval windows but the church was largely rebuilt in the early 19th century and then restored again in 1898-1899.

Beverley Westwood is open pasture with unusual bylaws. When, about 1258, the town burgesses gave up their rights in the Archbishop of York's Beverley Parks, they received new rights on the Westwood. Later, in 1380, Archbishop Neville granted the land to the town for an annual rent of £5 a year. Freedom of movement was guaranteed to all who visited the area.

Beverley Parks was developed as a deer park when the Archbishop of York acquired the area c.1258. The venture lasted some 300 years but by 1574 the land had become 'disparked'. The Warton family later bought the property and brought back the deer but the estate was spilt up in 1725.

The Millennium Orchard aims to conserve traditional varieties of northern apple and to demonstrate traditional orchard management. In 2000 the first trees were planted. Some of the varieties thriving today include the wonderfully named Dogsnout and Bloody Ploughman. The latter is named after an unfortunate ploughman who was caught stealing apples and promptly shot by the gamekeeper. The Fillingham Pippin (from nearby Swanland) and the Hornsea Herring are both particularly rare but at the time of writing are thriving in the orchard.

Risby is the site of a deserted village and also the site of three lost country houses. The first house probably lay to the NW of Park Farm and the second was built in the mid-1680s at Risby but further to the south. This was a fine building with impressive terraced gardens on five levels, two pavilions and an ornamental pond. At a later date a large lake was laid out to the east along with a Gothic folly.

The house was apparently destroyed by fire in the 1770s. It was rebuilt but again badly damaged by fire less than ten years later and after that the remaining parts of the building were demolished.

Remains of the terraces can be clearly seen today from Dunflat Road.

ALPHABETTING IN EAST YORKSHIRE

Special Interest – Walk K

Spurn Head is a sand and shingle spit nearly 3.5 miles long with sand dunes colonised mainly by marram grass and sea buckthorn. It receives its material from the boulder clay ('till') that is eroded from the cliffs of Holderness to the north and is then transported southwards by longshore drift. As the Holderness coast continues to be eroded by the sea and so is pushed back westwards, Spurn Head, attached to Holderness, gets continually moved westwards as well.

It is believed that the spit goes through a cycle of erosion and deposition. The last complete cycle occurred between 1608 and 1849. In 1608 the spit was breached and the south end became an island. Gradually the spit began to develop again until the sea broke through once more in 1849. This left the spit looking, at high tide, like a string of small islets with 'Spurn Island' now a separate feature at the south-west end.

Concern was expressed over the possible interference with shipping lanes in the Humber estuary and the threat to the lighthouses on Spurn Island. Great efforts were therefore made to protect and to strengthen the spit. Between 1870 and 1960 both groynes and revetments were added and these seem to have helped stabilise the spit and helped it to regain its bulbous tip.

Facing Europe, Spurn Head occupies an important strategic position in war-time and during the First World War a rail line was constructed along the spit. In the Second World War the present concrete road was built but the spit was still vulnerable to a storm surge in 1942 that undermined the rail line. Therefore, as further protection, a concrete seawall was constructed.

The display at the Visitor Centre explains how current thinking favours the idea that the spit should not be controlled by hard concrete defences but should be allowed to develop naturally under the influence of the waves. The sea should be left to wash sand up and over the ridge, so letting it move gradually westwards.

Spurn is now a National Nature Reserve and coastal defences have generally not been maintained. It is thought that the spit is probably longer now than it has ever been.

Ravenser and Ravenser Odd are two of the many villages that the 'Hidden Holderness' research group have identified as having been lost to the North Sea and the waters of the Humber Estuary. Ravenser once stood at the end of Spurn Point. It was from here that the Danish army beaten at Stamford Bridge in 1066 left England and also the place where Henry Bolingbroke landed in 1399 before defeating Richard II to become Henry IV.

However, during the 13th century, a second village, known as Ravenser Odd, developed and began trading with passing ships, much to the dismay of Hull and Grimsby. By the 1260s it had its own mayor and later it sent representatives to Parliament. Yet Ravenser Odd's history was short-lived because by the late 1300s the North Sea was eroding the island that it had created in the first place. Tales of Odd's last days recall bodies being washed out of graves and the island becoming a pirates' den before it finally sank below the waves around 1366. Ravenser itself was lost the following century.

Spurn has had a number of **lighthouses**. Nothing remains of the two towers built in 1675 by Justinian Angell. The remains of the circular wall surrounding John Smeaton's lighthouse of 1776 is still visible and the stump of the Low Lighthouse (1852) on the tidal flats is obvious. The High Lighthouse, erected in 1895, has been disused since 1985.

Kilnsea possesses one the country's concrete **acoustical sound mirrors** which were designed around the time of World War I to give early warning of the approach of enemy aircraft. The mirror worked by focusing the noise of aircraft engines on to a mobile microphone which amplified the sound. Relatively slow moving aircraft and airships could be detected before they came into view. Kilnsea's mirror is located between Kilnsea Grange and the North Sea. Acoustic mirrors became obsolete with the development of radar.

Old Kilnsea (not to be confused with the present settlement) was lost to the sea soon after 1852.

Bull Sand Fort lies two miles offshore to the SW and was built in World War I but was also manned throughout the Second World War.

WALK K
Kilnsea

Map: Explorer 292
S.E.P.:   Kilnsea car park (417158)
Bus: No bus service
Longer walk distance: **8.9 miles**
Shorter walks: any out-and-back from Kilnsea
Special interest:
         Spurn Head, Lost villages

Kilnsea 'pool near the kiln'

Ravenser Odd 'headland near Ravenser'

Spurn Head (compare with Shakespeare's 'Rauenspurgh') replaced older 'Ravenser Odd', 'spur' meaning a projection of land

This walk does, of course, allow the reason for visiting one of Britain's best known NNRs and an internationally important bird sanctuary. The Humber is one of Europe's most important estuaries for wildlife and has 'European Marine Site' designation.

To provide variation along the walk it is suggested that the route out to the tip of Spurn Point takes the east side of the spit along the North Sea shoreline whilst the return walk uses the variety of trails through the sand dunes on the Humber estuary side of the spit.

We start from the car park at the Crown and Anchor pub (1) in Kilnsea but first pause

to check the excellent information boards at the car park. From here we then follow the pavement eastwards, past the now-closed St Helen's Church, to the former Blue Bell pub, now the Spurn Visitor Centre (2). Wall plaques indicate the rates of coastal erosion.

Walking through the Visitor Centre car park, we follow the fingerpost directing us on to the Spurn Path. At first we walk on the top of the low Holderness boulder clay cliff. When we reach Kilnsea Warren (3) and the start of the sand and shingle spit, it will be easier to walk on the beach.

We pass the remains of former groynes and the jumbled mass of concrete blocks that show the damage that North Sea storms can do to coastal defences.

As we continue towards the High Lighthouse we have the opportunity not only to observe some of the area's rich bird life but also to admire the wonderful variety of coloured pebbles under our feet. If we look out to sea, we can imagine the position of the old villages of Ravenser and Ravenser Odd before they were destroyed by the waves.

Approaching the bulbous end of Spurn Point, we spot a small green-coned weather station tower in the dunes on our right. When we first investigated this area in mid-April, we found the surrounding sea-buckthorn shrubs covered in the cocoons of what we assumed were brown-tail moths with their young caterpillars still wriggling inside.

Continuing on round the tip of the spit, we enter the Humber estuary and pass the concrete remains of wartime fortifications. We note, too, the lifeboat moored at the end of the jetty. On account of the history of shipping disasters along the North Sea coast, this is a permanently manned lifeboat and is said to be the only one in the country operated in this way.

On the beach adjacent to the car park at (4) we see the remnant of the old Low Lighthouse and from the car park we now follow the fingerpost indicating the public footpath. This path through the dunes is more pleasant than the road, although we will have to use the road for a short stretch when the dune path disappears.

We regain the path which leads on to the Chalk Bank at (5). This is the sea defence completed in 1855 to close the breach caused by an earlier storm. We must see the Heliogoland Trap, a large cage-like structure for catching birds that will be ringed, recorded and then released. Highland cattle seem unconcerned as we pass by.

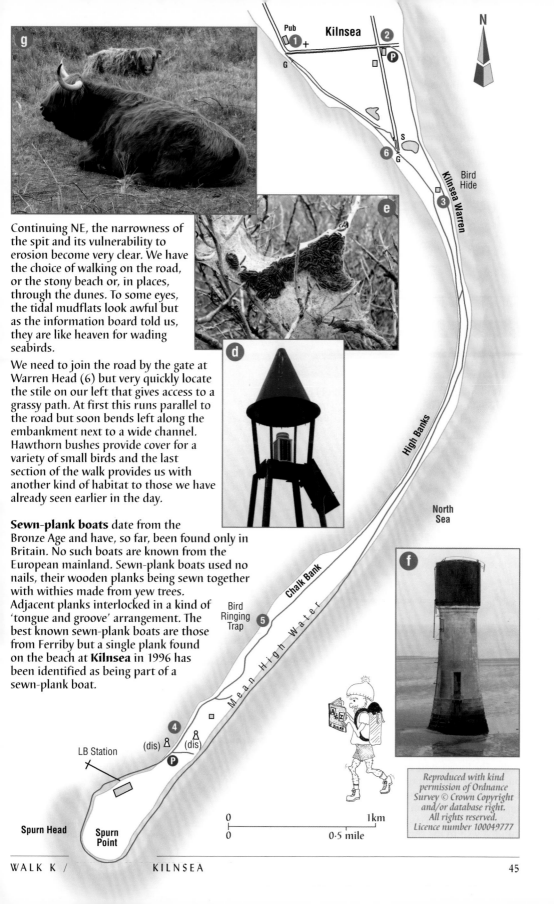

Continuing NE, the narrowness of the spit and its vulnerability to erosion become very clear. We have the choice of walking on the road, or the stony beach or, in places, through the dunes. To some eyes, the tidal mudflats look awful but as the information board told us, they are like heaven for wading seabirds.

We need to join the road by the gate at Warren Head (6) but very quickly locate the stile on our left that gives access to a grassy path. At first this runs parallel to the road but soon bends left along the embankment next to a wide channel. Hawthorn bushes provide cover for a variety of small birds and the last section of the walk provides us with another kind of habitat to those we have already seen earlier in the day.

Sewn-plank boats date from the Bronze Age and have, so far, been found only in Britain. No such boats are known from the European mainland. Sewn-plank boats used no nails, their wooden planks being sewn together with withies made from yew trees. Adjacent planks interlocked in a kind of 'tongue and groove' arrangement. The best known sewn-plank boats are those from Ferriby but a single plank found on the beach at **Kilnsea** in 1996 has been identified as being part of a sewn-plank boat.

WALK L
Lockington and Lund

Maps: Explorer 294 and 295
S.E.P.: St Mary's, Lockington (997468)
Bus: 121 Scarborough-Hull
Longer walk distance: **9.9 miles**
Shorter walk alternative: **7.2 miles**
Special interest:
  Four villages, Watton Priory

and village cross are recommended before we retrace steps to the gate at (6).

A clear path should be visible going diagonally over the cropland, through a gap in the hedge and on to the corner of Lund Moor Wood (7). From

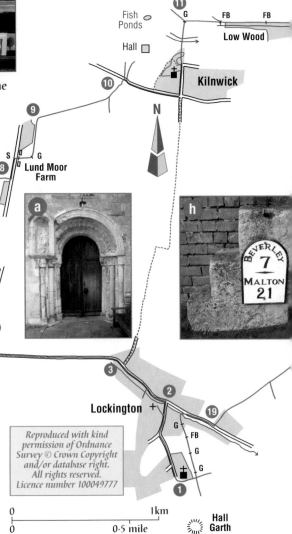

The walk starts from St Mary's Church (1) at the south end of Lockington village. We go north along Church Lane, turn right at the T-junction and come to the centre of the village (2). Crossing over the stream known locally as 'The Beck' we turn left on Front Street and walk beside the beck with its numerous fords and footbridges.

At Kilnwick Lane (3) the shorter walk turns right. The longer walk heads on towards Lund and at the T-junction turns right for 200m to the road bend (4). Turning left, we leave the tarmac and walk round two field edges to join Lockington Road (5) where we go left into Lund. A visit to the church, pub, old smithy

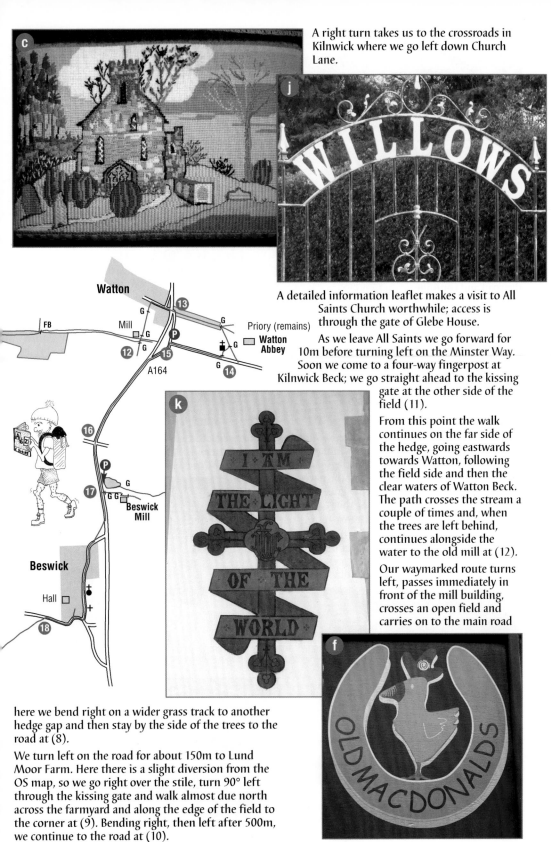

A right turn takes us to the crossroads in Kilnwick where we go left down Church Lane.

A detailed information leaflet makes a visit to All Saints Church worthwhile; access is through the gate of Glebe House.

As we leave All Saints we go forward for 10m before turning left on the Minster Way. Soon we come to a four-way fingerpost at Kilnwick Beck; we go straight ahead to the kissing gate at the other side of the field (11).

From this point the walk continues on the far side of the hedge, going eastwards towards Watton, following the field side and then the clear waters of Watton Beck. The path crosses the stream a couple of times and, when the trees are left behind, continues alongside the water to the old mill at (12).

Our waymarked route turns left, passes immediately in front of the mill building, crosses an open field and carries on to the main road here we bend right on a wider grass track to another hedge gap and then stay by the side of the trees to the road at (8).

We turn left on the road for about 150m to Lund Moor Farm. Here there is a slight diversion from the OS map, so we go right over the stile, turn 90° left through the kissing gate and walk almost due north across the farmyard and along the edge of the field to the corner at (9). Bending right, then left after 500m, we continue to the road at (10).

through Watton village. We turn right and come to the A164 road at (13).

Here we cross straight over the road and continue along a wide path. When we reach a gate, the path splits. Ahead of us is the path to the remains of Watton Abbey but we take the path bending right and aim towards Watton Church. We soon swing left to the gate at the NE corner of the churchyard and going through this gate we can visit the church and then, leaving by the south door, come out on to the road at (14).

Turning right, we follow the road to the T-junction (15) and go left on the side road to join the A164. Bearing left, we now follow the main road towards Beverley. We can use either the pavement on the right-hand side or the wide grass verge on the left and we continue, past the crossroads (16), to the parking spot and p.r.o.w. at (17).

At this point it is worth taking the trouble to turn left on the track and do a short out-and-back detour to Beswick Mill. We can expect a cheery welcome from the wonderful variety of

wildfowl living around the farm and, sitting beside the mill pond, there are more birds to spot before we return on the track to the A164.

Turning left, we cross the road, use the pavement and bend right into Beswick. Main Street leads us through the settlement, past Beswick Hall, the church and the chapel, to the lane called Beswick Heads. We turn right, twist left and right, then leave the lane at the path indicator on our left (18).

Waymarked gaps in the hedges lead us across five fields, along the side of another field and down a wide path into Lockington village (19).

For the last stage of the walk, we turn right on Front Street, go left at the Minster Way fingerpost (next to no. 37), follow the path to

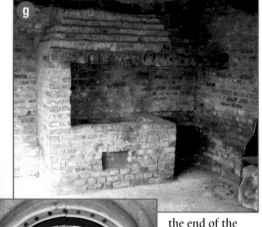

the end of the houses and continue over pasture land with the beck a little way over to our right. At the trees, we go right over the footbridge and back to St Mary's Church.

Special Interest – Walk L

Lockington 'Loca's farm'
Lund 'grove' (sometimes 'sanctuary wood')
Kilnwick ('Killik') 'Cylla's dairy-farm'
Watton 'wet, saturated hillside'
Beswick ('Bezzik') 'Besi's dairy-farm'

St Mary's Church, Lockington dates from about 1150 but has had numerous extensions and alterations since then. Pevsner & Neave describe it as 'one of the most enthralling churches in the East Riding'. After the Norman Conquest, Nigel Fossard was given the manor of Lockington and he built a wooden castle a short distance to the south of the present church. It was his grandson, William Fossard, who built the stone church and the Norman doorway is still visible today. At some time, probably in the 14th century, the door arch was radically altered in order to install the niche we see on the left side.

One of the more remarkable features of the church is the collection in the south chapel of 173 coats of arms. These trace the ancestry of the Estoft family as Lords of the Manor since the times of the Fossards. The shields were repainted in 1851 but, apparently, there are a number of heraldic errors. Several of the coats contain arms to which the owners were not entitled and there are numerous mistakes in colouring. But you need to be an expert to find the mistakes!

In the churchyard Reverend Johannes Witty's tomb, repaired in 2005, is a rare example of a brick and stone funeral monument.

All Saints Church, Lund is mainly a 14th century building but there is documentary evidence of a church being in existence from at least the late 12th century and the font is of Norman date. The two damaged effigies in the chancel commemorate Edmund Thwaites (died 1500) and his wife Joan. The Thwaites were Lords of the Manor.

All Saints Church, Kilnwick has a Norman foundation but, like many of the other churches we visit, has seen extensive alterations. Among numerous interesting features, the church has a pig's head carving in the arch above the main door, banners made of zinc foil on either side of the east window and a fine oak pulpit bought from Beverley Minster for £3.3s in 1726.

Watton Priory stood just to the north of St Mary's Church. About 1150 Eustace Fitzjohn founded a house here for the Gilbertine religious order which had been established ten years earlier at Sempringham in Lincolnshire. Watton was the largest of the 26 Gilbertine houses in England and, like half of the houses, was a nunnery served by male canons. There were therefore two separate areas, one for the nuns and one for the canons. Although the double house shared the same Priory Church, there was a wall in the church dividing the men from the women so that they could not see each other.

Between the male and female sections of the priory stood the Prior's Lodging. This is the impressive building, now known as Watton Abbey, that faces us as we walk from Watton village. It became a private house when Henry VIII dissolved the priory in 1539.

St Mary's Church, Watton is of uncertain date but it may have been constructed using material from the adjacent priory when it was dissolved.

Beswick Water Mill is a delightful sight. It seems that watermills have stood here for about 1,000 years. A replacement for an earlier mill was constructed around 1600 and this, in turn, was rebuilt around 1803. The mill used water power from the ponds for milling grain and it remained active until the 1960s.

The ponds are fed by local springs and attract a wide variety of birds, both resident and migratory. The farm is also home to a number of domesticated birds as well as some endangered animal species.

St Margaret's Church, Beswick was built for Lord Hotham in 1871 to replace a thatched medieval building – the village had already been bought by the Hotham family in 1838. Opposite to the church is the impressive brick manor house of Beswick Hall dating from about 1600.

WALK M
Millington

Map: Explorer 294
S.E.P.:   St Margaret's, Millington (830518)
Bus: No bus service; use Pocklington
Longer walk (excl Lily Dale):   **9.9 miles**
Shorter NE loop: **4.5 miles**
Shorter SW loop: **6.8 miles**
Special interest:
     Millington Pastures

This walk forms a figure-of-eight and we start in Millington where we decide either to do the full walk or just one of the two loops.

From St Margaret's Church (1) we walk NE along the road called Wood Gate towards Millington Wood in Lily Dale (2). Here there is the option of doing an out-and-back visit to the end of the woodland track.

We then continue on the road that runs along Millington Dale, past (3), to the Wolds Way Link path fingerpost at (4)*. Turning right through the gate, we make for the Wolds Way itself at another gate 70m straight ahead of us. We need at first to take the path on the far side of the fence as we turn sharp right to go up the hillside, with the fence now on our right. For the next three miles we shall be following the Wolds Way and walking beside prehistoric earthworks for parts of the trail.

The route is clearly waymarked and there are fine views down to Millington Dale and back to the superb interlocking spurs of Frendal Dale. We should be prepared for the steep descent into Sylvan Dale (5). However, the climb on the opposite side of this dry valley is less fearsome as we make our way diagonally up across the course of an old Roman road to a small gate and round to the field corner at (6). We then continue to Warren Farm, the home of two proud peacocks.

The path skirts left of the farmstead and very quickly the short walk turns right over the stile in the hedge (7) and goes down the hill and back into Millington.

The longer walk carries straight on, before twisting left, right and right again (8) to follow the wide track down alongside Warrendale Plantation.

When we come to the metalled road (9) the Wolds Way turns left but we continue straight ahead. We pass the driveways to Kilnwick Percy Hall (well worth seeing if there is time) and Kilnwick Percy Golf Club before

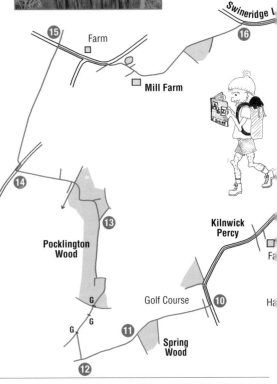

we get to the footpath at (10). Here we leave the road and turn off right over the golf course.

Crossing a tarred driveway, we aim for the right-hand edge of Spring Wood ahead of us. At the trees, we keep to the side of the wood and come to the waymarker post in the hedge-line at (11). We take the narrow path between the hedge and fence to the fingerpost at (12) where we turn sharp right to the telecommunications mast.

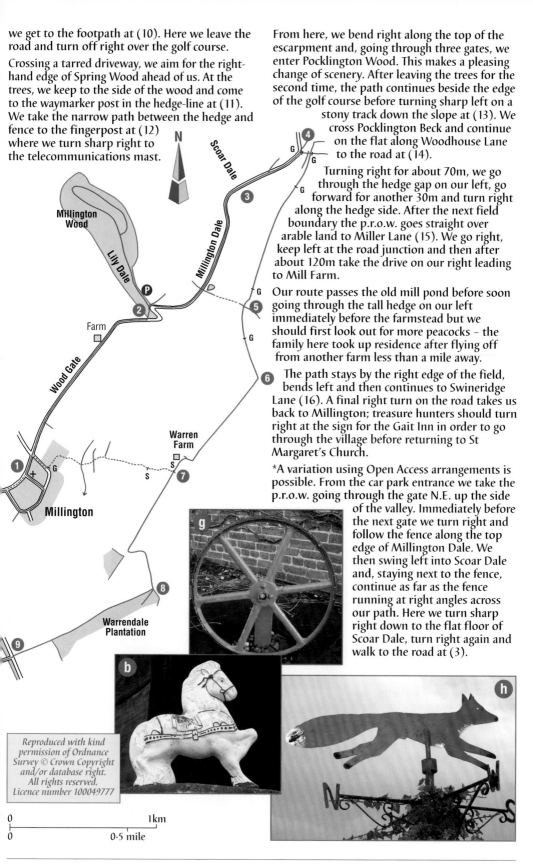

From here, we bend right along the top of the escarpment and, going through three gates, we enter Pocklington Wood. This makes a pleasing change of scenery. After leaving the trees for the second time, the path continues beside the edge of the golf course before turning sharp left on a stony track down the slope at (13). We cross Pocklington Beck and continue on the flat along Woodhouse Lane to the road at (14).

Turning right for about 70m, we go through the hedge gap on our left, go forward for another 30m and turn right along the hedge side. After the next field boundary the p.r.o.w. goes straight over arable land to Miller Lane (15). We go right, keep left at the road junction and then after about 120m take the drive on our right leading to Mill Farm.

Our route passes the old mill pond before soon going through the tall hedge on our left immediately before the farmstead but we should first look out for more peacocks – the family here took up residence after flying off from another farm less than a mile away.

The path stays by the right edge of the field, bends left and then continues to Swineridge Lane (16). A final right turn on the road takes us back to Millington; treasure hunters should turn right at the sign for the Gait Inn in order to go through the village before returning to St Margaret's Church.

*A variation using Open Access arrangements is possible. From the car park entrance we take the p.r.o.w. going through the gate N.E. up the side of the valley. Immediately before the next gate we turn right and follow the fence along the top edge of Millington Dale. We then swing left into Scoar Dale and, staying next to the fence, continue as far as the fence running at right angles across our path. Here we turn sharp right down to the flat floor of Scoar Dale, turn right again and walk to the road at (3).

Special Interest – Walk M

Millington probably 'farmstead of Midele'

Kilnwick Percy 'dairy-farm of Cylla (or Cylla and his people)'. This place was linked with the Percy family from the 12th century.

Pocklington 'Pocela's farm'

Millington Pastures Before the enclosure of the land in the 1960s, over 400 acres was common pasture and was shared by the local farmers. Each farmer rented a number of 'gaits' or 'stints', one gait representing enough pasture for six sheep. The Pastures had a total of 108 gaits.

Millington Wood in Lily Dale was declared a Local Nature Reserve in 1991 and is part of the Millington Wood and Pastures SSSI. It has been described as botanically the richest woodland in the East Riding. Of particular importance is the ash woodland which dates back to the Middle Ages and although the development in the 1960s of commercial forestry for beech and spruce resulted in the felling of many of the ash trees, a small area of the ancient woodland was left untouched. Wild garlic and bluebells give a colourful ground cover in spring and giant bellflowers can grow to nearly two metres tall. The circular metal structure in the wood is a kiln for making charcoal.

Way Post Sculptures

A series of eleven oak posts has been installed at three locations in Millington Dale. Each post has its own carved letter and together these form the message 'GAIT IN WOLDS'. The way posts are a reminder of the former gaits of pasture land and also tell us that Millington Dale is one of the gateways into the Wolds. Each post has carvings that show us features of the surrounding landscape and all the posts have a hitching ring to which animals could have been tethered. The Way Post project was started by Lis Molzahn and Paul Brooks.

St Margaret's Church, Millington dates back to Norman times and includes zigzagged arches above the south doorway. Inside the Church is a new stained glass window showing the Journey to Emmaus. Jesus is walking with two of his dejected followers who are unaware that he has been raised from death and oblivious that their companion is the Risen Lord himself. The Christian life is often portrayed as a walk or journey with Jesus as our companion and the scenery in the stained glass shows the area around Millington, so popular with walkers.

Outside the Church are two cross bases that are thought to be medieval. One has been inscribed as a sundial.

Kilnwick Percy is the site of a small village finally deserted in the early 18th century with only the church and hall still remaining. Kilnwick Percy Hall looks resplendent in its parkland setting. However, none of the original 1574 building is still standing and many of the later developments were demolished in 1947-49. What remains today includes the especially impressive portico, with its four Grecian-style columns, which forms a 'porte-cochere' or entrance big enough to allow a carriage to draw up under cover. In rainy weather passengers could dismount without getting wet.

The Hall is now in the hands of a Buddhist community of over 30 residents. Visitors are welcome to view the mansion and to explore the surrounding gardens and woodland.

A Roman site has been excavated about half a mile NE of Millington and fragments of pavement, tiles, coins and pottery suggest this may have been the site of a villa.

Way Post Sculptures

Special Interest – Walk N

Nafferton 'Nattfari (the night traveller)'s farm'

Wansford 'Wandel's ford'

Skerne village was named after the stream (Skerne Beck). Skerne could have meant 'bright, clear' or it could have meant 'cleansing, healing, baptism' so the river might have been 'the cleansing, healing river'

Driffield (not 'dry') possibly 'stubble' plus 'open country' (feld)

Nafferton is the home of 'The Naffers', a series of springs emerging from the chalk in and around Nafferton and helping to feed the village pond. This was once a mill pond supplying water power to the adjacent corn mill. This closed in 1986. The steam mill of 1858, built close to the railway station, was only demolished in 2005-6 and the land has been redeveloped for housing.

One interesting feature of the village is the number of 18th century houses with datestones. At least nine have been recorded, most of which also have the initials of the first owner and his wife.

All Saints Church, like others on the Alphabet Walks, is built on an obvious raised mound and this may indicate a pre-Christian worship site. However, the present church still retains its original Norman chancel arch and font and there is a Norman-French inscription on the outside south face of the tower. Translated this reads: 'God help the Church and save the Kingdom'. A later wall-tablet inside the building records that Ann Esh had '... such a happy talent for learning that at four years of age she was capable, punctually, to read a chapter of the Bible'.

Wansford in the late 18th century was a bustling industrial village with a huge carpet factory, owned by Sir Christopher Sykes, employing some 400 people. The factory was built between the Driffield Canal and the River Hull. Carpet making finished in the 1820s but the building was not demolished until the 20th century.

St Mary's Church is another Sykes church and was built in the 1860s. Probably its most outstanding feature is the Italian Gothic style screen made of marble, alabaster and iron.

Skerne village includes at its west end the house called Rose Cottage. High on its wall are the initials R.A.. These are said to be those of Richard Arkwright whose father, of the same name, invented the water-powered spinning frame. This was one of the most important inventions of the Industrial Revolution. Richard, junior, bought the Skerne estate in 1792 and the family rebuilt much of the village and surrounding farms.

St Leonard's Church has a surprising interior and contains considerable Norman remains in both the nave and chancel. However, expect a shock as we enter the church; the stone monuments, say Pevsner & Neave, have been grotesquely retooled and may give us a fright!

Driffield advertises itself as 'The Capital of the Wolds'. It had a royal castle in the 1200s but from the 1700s the town developed as a market centre for the farm produce of the surrounding area. The town's fortunes were boosted in 1767 by the cutting of a canal from Riverhead to link the town with the River Hull. This eased the movement of grain and the large former warehouses we see today indicate the scale of earlier farming activities.

The arrival of the railway in 1846 gave considerable competition but by reducing toll charges the canal managed to compete successfully until the early 20th century. Today it is used by leisure craft.

Bell Mills used water power from a local stream and was built on the south side of the town in 1792 to manufacture textiles and carpets. Rebuilt in the 1950s, it now mills wheat for making into flour for bread and biscuits.

WALK N
Nafferton

Map: Explorer 295
S.E.P.:   Riverhead, Driffield (029571)
Bus: 121 Scarborough-Hull
Longer walk (via Skerne):   **9.9 miles**
Shorter walk (B1249 & Canal):   **7.4 miles**
Special interest:
       Driffield Canal

This walk is one which allows us to see something of Driffield as well as Nafferton.

We start from the end of the old Driffield Canal (1). Rather confusingly, this is called Riverhead but there is adequate space for car parking and it is close to the railway station.

Walking to the road called River Head, we turn right and go to the B1249 road junction, turn right again and branch first left down Meadow Road.

This suburban road becomes a track and we are led beside the railway, then over it, and continue between the trees, beside a field and through more trees to the gate at (2). The path carries on straight ahead, crosses a ditch and turns left, comes to the corner of the field and goes right, then comes to the road at (3). From here we carry on in the same direction along Markman Lane into Nafferton.

Immediately before All Saints Church (4) we take the path on our left which leads us round to High Street at (5). We go right, right again at the Methodist Church and arrive back at the parish church.

We continue down Priestgate beside the large pond. Where the road turns sharp right (6) we go on ahead through the gate in front of us.

From here we need to steer very slightly to our left to locate the gate in the opposite field corner. Now we follow Nafferton Beck to the railway line. Crossing carefully, we walk beside

DRIFFIELD

Bell Mills

Skerne Hil

the stream for about 1.5 miles into Wansford, noting that we need to change from left to right bank at the road leading to Wansford Church (7).

At the main road (8) we have a dilemma. The short walk turns right and goes for a mile along the B1249 beside the Driffield Canal. At busy times this stretch is certainly not pleasant and one option is to use the bus or a second car to return to Driffield. However, there is the attraction of allowing us to use the canal-side path on the other side of the road when we reach Whinhill Lock (9). From here the path takes us all the way back to River Head. The waterway is an SSSI and as well as observing the birds on the canal to our right, we get frequent views of the swans on the River Hull (or West Beck as it is also called in this section) over to our left.

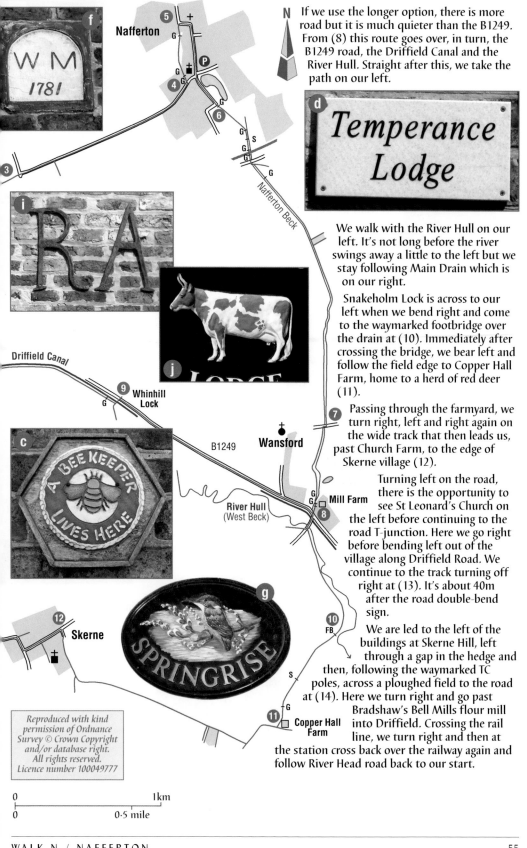

f
W M
1781

Nafferton
5 +
G

G P
4 G

G
6

G S
G
G
G

Nafferton Beck

3

i
R A

j
LODGE

d
Temperance Lodge

If we use the longer option, there is more road but it is much quieter than the B1249. From (8) this route goes over, in turn, the B1249 road, the Driffield Canal and the River Hull. Straight after this, we take the path on our left.

We walk with the River Hull on our left. It's not long before the river swings away a little to the left but we stay following Main Drain which is on our right.

Snakeholm Lock is across to our left when we bend right and come to the waymarked footbridge over the drain at (10). Immediately after crossing the bridge, we bear left and follow the field edge to Copper Hall Farm, home to a herd of red deer (11).

Driffield Canal

9 Whinhill
G Lock

c
A BEE KEEPER LIVES HERE

B1249

Wansford

7 Passing through the farmyard, we turn right, left and right again on the wide track that then leads us, past Church Farm, to the edge of Skerne village (12).

G
G Mill Farm
River Hull
(West Beck)
8

Turning left on the road, there is the opportunity to see St Leonard's Church on the left before continuing to the road T-junction. Here we go right before bending left out of the village along Driffield Road. We continue to the track turning off right at (13). It's about 40m after the road double-bend sign.

g
SPRINGRISE

12
Skerne

10
FB

S

We are led to the left of the buildings at Skerne Hill, left through a gap in the hedge and then, following the waymarked TC poles, across a ploughed field to the road at (14). Here we turn right and go past Bradshaw's Bell Mills flour mill into Driffield. Crossing the rail line, we turn right and then at the station cross back over the railway again and follow River Head road back to our start.

G

11
Copper Hall Farm

0   1km
0   0·5 mile

WALK O
Owthorne

Map: Explorer 292
S.E.P.T.: North Promenade (342281)
Buses: 75, 76, 77 from Hull
Longer walk (incl Tunstall): **11.4 miles**
Medium walk (via Thirtle Bridge): **7.3 miles**
Shorter walk (via Waxholme): **4.2 miles**
Special interest:
    Lost coastal villages

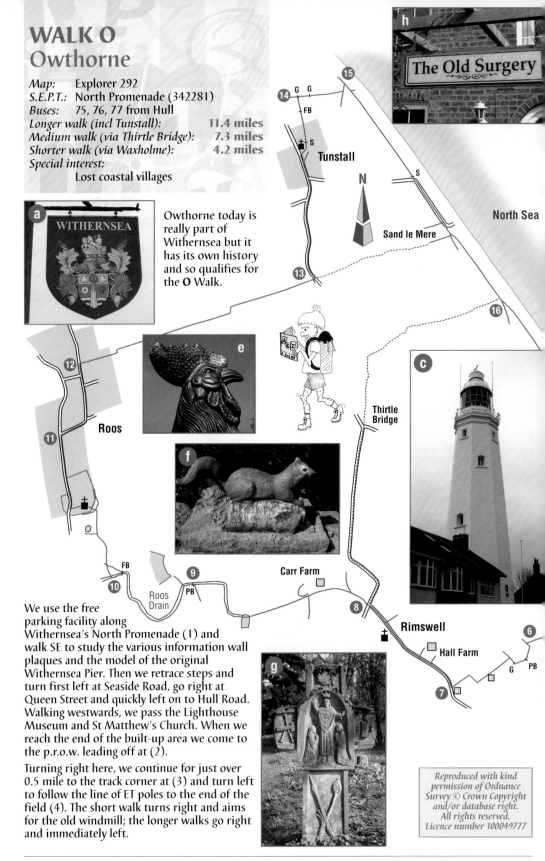

h The Old Surgery

a WITHERNSEA

Owthorne today is really part of Withernsea but it has its own history and so qualifies for the **O** Walk.

15

14 G G
FB

13

Tunstall

N

Sand le Mere

North Sea

16

12

e

Roos

11

f

c

Thirtle Bridge

10 FB
9 PB
Roos Drain

Carr Farm

8

Rimswell

Hall Farm
6
G PB
7

g

We use the free parking facility along Withernsea's North Promenade (1) and walk SE to study the various information wall plaques and the model of the original Withernsea Pier. Then we retrace steps and turn first left at Seaside Road, go right at Queen Street and quickly left on to Hull Road. Walking westwards, we pass the Lighthouse Museum and St Matthew's Church. When we reach the end of the built-up area we come to the p.r.o.w. leading off at (2).

Turning right here, we continue for just over 0.5 mile to the track corner at (3) and turn left to follow the line of ET poles to the end of the field (4). The short walk turns right and aims for the old windmill; the longer walks go right and immediately left.

ALPHABETTING IN EAST YORKSHIRE

Soon there's another sharp right turn and then a plank bridge over a ditch before we swing left to the area called Rimswell Valley (5).

Staying next to the hedge, we curve round left beside a ditch at the path junction (6). We are directed right over another plank bridge, then right again after the gate at the end of the field. A little further on we turn left along a drive made of unusual concrete slabs and are led round to Church Road at (7).

A right turn takes us through Rimswell (treasure clue hunters check the churchyard) and up to the road junction at (8). Here the middle distance walk goes right; the long walk crosses straight over and takes the driveway to 'K Fresh', the large egg-producing unit at Carr Farm.

At the end of the farm, waymarks direct us straight on across ploughland and through the edge of a small clump of trees before we bend right and continue on a wide grassy path with a ditch on our right. At this stage of the walk we are aware of the gently rolling landscape of the Holderness boulder clay.

We avoid turning left on to the obvious track by the hedge at (9) but instead continue ahead over the plank bridge for another 90m to the Roos Drain. Turning left, we follow this wide ditch and come round to the footbridge at (10). We go over the bridge and follow the path, crossing right over the ditch where the track bends left, to Roos Church. A gap in the hedge gives access to the churchyard.

We leave the church by the west end, turn right on the road and walk into Roos. There's much for treasure hunters to see as we go through the village, turning right at Lamb Lane (11), left at the road junction and continuing to the Roos Arms pub at (12).

Opposite the pub we take the signed p.r.o.w. towards Sand le Mere. Fenced at first, this path goes in an almost direct line (with just two left-right jiggles) between the houses and then along fieldsides to Southfield Lane (13).

Here we turn left and follow the hedged, twisting lane into Tunstall. At All Saints Church the path goes through the churchyard to the stile in the far right-hand corner. Crossing the stile, we turn right for just 10m and then go sharp left to follow the fence. There's another stile, a footbridge and a short length of double-hedged path as we continue to the track at (14). One final right turn brings us to the coast (15).

From here back to our start it's about 3.5 miles along the edge of the North Sea. The coast is being constantly eroded and the path now runs along the cliff edge. Great care must obviously be taken to avoid unstable sections. If the tide is out, it will be possible to walk some stretches along the beach, provided a safe descent of the cliffs can be found.

Reading the notice at Sand le Mere we are told that this is the place where the Greenwich Meridian line (longitude 0°) first enters the U.K. from the North Pole.

At Tunstall Drain (16) we need to bear left towards the sea, rather than continue on the wide track going ahead to Redhouse Farm. When we pass the edge of Waxholme, we note that Cliff Farm, shown on the OS map, has now disappeared as a result of marine erosion.

As we come to Owthorne, we pass a large open grass area, then walk beside the houses and drop down to the North Promenade. We finish the walk further along the sea front.

xholme

5
PB
3
4

Owthorne

1

Pier Towers

Hull Road

WITHERNSEA

B1362
2

0   1km
0   0·5 mile

Special Interest – Walk O

Owthorne 'the remote thorn tree'

Waxholme probably 'farm noted for its bees' (i.e., the wax)

Tunstall not clear; possibly 'farmstead'

Roos possibly 'moor, heath'

Rimswell probably 'Rim's well'

Withernsea 'withern' perhaps means 'near the thorn tree' and 'sea' refers to 'pool or lake'.

Lost Coastal Villages are an important feature of this walk. The research group 'Hidden Holderness' records that settlements at Sand le Mere, Waxholme, Owthorne, Newsham and Old Withernsea have all disappeared as a result of coastal erosion.

The main reason for the high rate of loss is that the boulder clay ('till') cliffs of the Holderness coast are geologically very weak and an easy prey to violent wave action.

Ada Pringle notes that, for the period 1852-1952, average rates of erosion on this stretch of coast have been calculated at 1.2m per year. However, there has been considerable variation, from less than 1.0m in the more sheltered north to 2.75m per year in the more exposed south near Kilnsea.

As a millennium project for 2000 AD, a Meridian Marker was erected at Tunstall in 2000. Only three years later it disappeared when the cliff collapsed.

Interpretation plaques along Withernsea Promenade tell the story of the churches of **Old Withernsea** and its neighbour, **Owthorne**. Two sisters wished to build a local church but they could not agree on the design of the building. As a result, separate churches were constructed, one with a tower and the other with a steeple. These became known as the Sister Kirkes.

Old Withernsea's church of St Mary (with the spire) was destroyed with the town in the 15th century but some of the salvaged stones were used in building the replacement St Nicholas' Church. Owthorne Church (with the tower) did not survive the great storm of 1816 and, although many bodies from the graveyard were transferred to **Rimswell Church**, body-snatchers from London were said to have come to steal corpses from the exhumed coffins. Rimswell Church is now closed.

Withernsea grew with the opening of the Hull and Holderness railway line in 1854 but ambitious plans for its greater development never materialised. Particularly disappointing was the story of the **iron pier,** with its brick twin entrance towers. Built in 1877, it suffered repeated storm damage before it was eventually dismantled around 1900. A replica model is on display on the promenade.

The **lighthouse**, built in the 1890s and located inland on Hull Road, is a prominent landmark. It stopped working in 1976 and is now a museum. The work of the Withernsea and Spurn lifeboat crews is amongst the descriptive exhibits.

Withernsea's **coastal defences** were strengthened 1995-97: the existing seawall was replaced with a new reinforced concrete wave return wall and large boulders from southern Norway were placed as rock armour to protect the lower part of the new wall.

St Nicholas' Church, Withernsea replaced St Mary's Church, destroyed by the sea in the 15th century. But in 1609 the new church, already badly neglected, lost its roof in a storm and was later abandoned as a ruin. Careful restoration in the 19th century rescued the building.

St Matthew's Church, Owthorne was built in the 1930s and replaced a chapel of ease on Queen Street North.

All Saints Church, Roos has a very unusual two-storey vestry, a tower built about 1442 using a legacy of 20 shillings, and a 'Calvary' cross carving near the church gate.

J.R.R. Tolkien, author of 'The Lord of the Rings', was billeted at The Old Rectory during the First World War. It is thought that whilst walking in local woods with his wife Edith and watching her dance for him, Tolkien received the inspiration for the tale of Beren (Tolkien himself) and Luthien (Edith) in the Silmarillion: 'as she danced ... he fell into an enchantment; for Luthien was the most beautiful of all the children of Iluvatar.'

All Saints Church, Tunstall is built mainly from rounded seashore cobbles which, although not particularly easy to build with, provided a cheap and easily accessible material. The church is first mentioned in 1115.

Special Interest – Walks P and U

The P and U Walks overlap at Kirby Underdale and so the Special Interest notes for the two walks are written here together.

A glance at the OS Geology map shows that both Painsthorpe and Uncleby lie at the junction of the Jurassic rocks with the Chalk Wolds and Kirby Underdale lies firmly in the Jurassic zone. This adds extra interest to the walks because we see more variety in the landscape. One thing that should be quickly apparent is the number of surface streams flowing generally westwards from springs issuing from the foot of the chalk. This is quite different to the dry valley landscapes we have seen on some of the Wolds walks.

Painsthorpe 'Paganus' outlying hamlet' (outlying from Kirby Underdale)

Painsthorpe Hall was built about 1815 for Admiral Sir Charles Richardson. From 1902-1906 it served as home for a group of Anglican Benedictine monks before they moved to Caldey Island in Pembrokeshire. The large cross visible from the footpath is one of several erected in the area by the Lords Halifax and commemorates their link with the Anglo-Catholic wing of the Anglican Church.

Kirby Underdale 'church farm in Hundle Dale or in Hundolf's valley'. The settlement is an estate village of Lord Halifax.

All Saints Church dates from around 1100 but shows evidence of numerous medieval alterations. Of special interest inside the building are the stained glass Jesse Tree window and the window commemorating the second Viscount Halifax. He is remembered for his attempts at the 'Malines Conversations' (1921-25) to reunite the Anglican and the Roman Catholic Churches.

A small Roman stone carving is said to depict the god Mercury.

On the outside of the church can be seen 12th century herring-bone carving on the tower and numerous pieces of medieval grave-slabs, mainly 13th century, built into the walls. Modern gravestones of the Halifax family make interesting reading, while the 14th century cross base reminds us of similar structures seen at Millington and Huggate. The cross base, looking like a stone chair, came from Stone Chair Close on Garrowby Street.

Uncleby 'Hunkel's farm'

Uncleby has only a few buildings, the most impressive of which is Manor House, a large 18th century farmhouse. Almost opposite and now in poor repair is the former Methodist

HALIFAX ESTATES

Chapel which was first built as a school for 'the poor children of Uncleby'. A little higher up the road can be seen the old village tap.

Bugthorpe 'Buggi's village'

Bugthorpe is another estate village of Lord Halifax. The houses and cottages were largely rebuilt in the 19th century but Freestone House on Main Street is unusual, dating from the late 18th century and being built of Jurassic limestone.

St Andrew's Church has a Norman font and chancel arch. The font is decorated with nailheads – reminders of Christ's crucifixion – and the arch contains a variety of interesting carvings. A major restoration of the church in 1936-37 was paid for by Lord Halifax.

Garrowby 'Gerwath's farm'

Garrowby Hall is home to the Earl of Halifax whose extensive Yorkshire landholdings are centred on the Garrowby Estate.

The first **Earl of Halifax** (1881-1959) held important political offices in the first half of the 20th century. He was, in turn, Viceroy of India, Foreign Secretary under Neville Chamberlain and Ambassador to the United States. It was once usual to dismiss Halifax as one of 'the guilty men' who, under Prime Minister Chamberlain, were responsible for the disastrous policy of appeasement towards Germany before the Second World War. Recently, however, historians have drawn a more subtle picture suggesting Halifax played a critical role in modifying Chamberlain's designs. There is evidence that many Labour leaders, the King and the majority of the Conservative Party would have preferred Halifax to Churchill as Chamberlain's successor. Halifax is buried at Kirby Underdale.

The present, third, Earl entertained the Queen at Garrowby during Ascot Week when the horse-racing event was temporarily transferred to York in 2005.

WALK P
Painsthorpe

Map: Explorer 294
S.E.P.: Wayrham picnic site (832567)
or in Kirby Underdale village
Bus: No bus service
Longer walk distance: **8.9 miles**
*Shorter walk (start at Kirby Underdale
and park second car at Wayrham):* **4.4 miles**
Special interest:
Kirby Underdale village

Painsthorpe today consists of only a couple of late 18th century farmhouses and an early 19th century Hall. However, the OS map also names Painsthorpe Lane, Field, Wold, Dale and **two** Painsthorpe Wold Farms, so there's reasonable justification for calling this the 'P' Walk! Moreover, we pass through some other delightfully sounding places: Worm Dale, Worsen Dale and Cheese Cake Wold so the walk also qualifies on the basis of its wonderful appellations.

down the slope and come to the bottom of Deep Dale. Crossing the stile, we follow the waymark and take the path bearing slightly left up the rough steps to the main track a little way up the slope. Now we bear right and climb steadily up the side of the valley to the gate at (5).

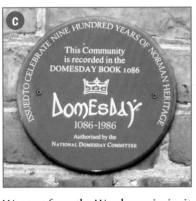

This Community
is recorded in the
DOMESDAY BOOK 1086

ISSUED TO CELEBRATE NINE HUNDRED YEARS OF NORMAN HERITAGE

DomEsday
1086-1986
Authorised by the
NATIONAL DOMESDAY COMMITTEE

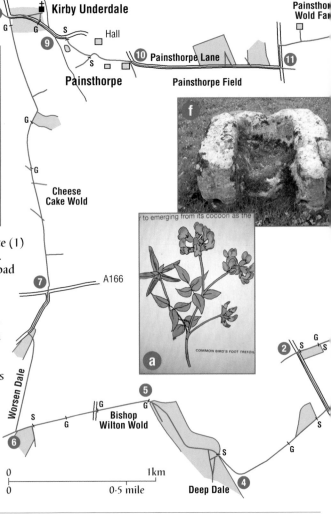

COMMON BIRD'S FOOT TREFOIL

We start from the Wayrham picnic site (1) on the side road adjacent to the A166. Going east on the Scenic Route side road to Huggate, we locate the fingerpost and stile on our right, just where the copse starts. We turn off here and at the next stile again turn right and use the concession allowing us to walk on the other (southerly) side of the hedge in order to avoid potentially boisterous cattle. From experience, it's a concession worth accepting.

When we reach the old Roman Road (2) we turn left and continue to the fingerpost at (3). This directs us right and along the top of the first of the day's steep-sided dry valleys.

Just before the transverse field boundary at (4), we turn right

The route turns left and follows the hedge-side over Bishop Wilton Wold, crosses Beacon Road and descends gently with fine views of the Vale of York, to the field corner at (6).

Here we turn sharp right and take the path between the double fence at the top of the steep side of Worsen Dale. Soon the path leads down through a few trees to Worsendale Road and we bear right up to the A166 road at (7).

Crossing carefully, we now follow the broad track, over Cheese Cake Wold, for a little over a mile to Kirby Underdale (8). Turning right, we go through the estate village

and, using the paved path just before the church, make sure we visit All Saints Church at the far end of the main street. There's much of historical interest both inside and outside the church building, including the grave of the Earl of Halifax, former Foreign Secretary.

We continue down the road a short way to the sharp left bend and the path leading off right (9). This takes us across an open field, from where we have excellent views on our left of Painsthorpe Hall. Crossing the stile at the other side of the field, we turn left and

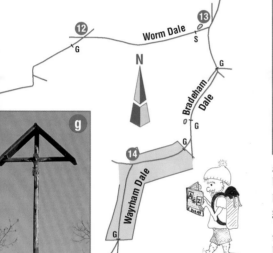

are led past the farm buildings that comprise Painsthorpe and up to Painsthorpe Lane (10).

Bearing right, we follow the lane as it climbs gently to the Roman Road at (11). We go left for 120m before turning right on the p.r.o.w. and then pass one of the two Painsthorpe Wold Farms on our left. The track turns left, then right along the further side of the hedge, before going through a gate and across a small field to the edge of Worm Dale (12).

The path slopes diagonally down the valley side to the floor of the dale and we continue to the field boundary and stile at the edge of Thixen Dale (13). On the other side of the stile we go forward for about 100m before turning sharp right to Bradeham Dale.

At the first gate, several paths converge; we stay on the valley floor. We pass a large dew pond and twist round to the fork in the track at (14). Here we bend left and continue between the trees up the gradual slope of Wayrham Dale to the A166 road. Following the indicators, we cross with care, go right for a few metres and then turn left on the grass path back to the car park.

WALK Q
Quintin Bottom

Map: Explorer 295
S.E.P.T.: Burton Agnes Hall (103631)
Bus: 121 Scarborough-Hull
Longer walk distance: **9.7 miles**
Shorter walk (uses bus or parked car to return
from Bracey Bridge to Burton Agnes): **4.8 miles**
Special interest:
Four villages, Burton Agnes Hall

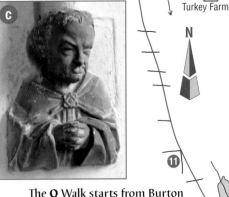

see the gap in the hedge at the far side of the field in front of us. Crossing this field, we come to Station Road (4).

Turning left, we walk for about 300m and take the path on our right. We are led over Kelk Beck and a mill race channel to a rather boggy patch of land. At this point the path may not be obvious; we go ahead veering slightly across to our right to the right-hand edge of a small conifer plantation.

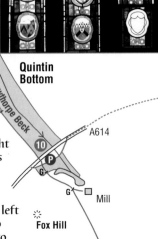

Kilham

Turkey Farm

N

Quintin Bottom

Lowthorpe Beck

A614

Harpham

Mill

Fox Hill

St Jo We

Drummer's Well

FB

The **Q** Walk starts from Burton Agnes Hall where there is free parking outside the stately home. It's a good idea to explore the adjacent Norman House and Church before the walk.

From the car park (1) we go down to the A614 and, ***crossing carefully***, turn right and walk to the fingerpost (2) directing us left off the road. Waymarked stiles, and the sight of Harpham Church tower, give us our line of direction across farmland to the edge of Harpham (3). Here we turn left to the crossroads and then go left again to complete a quick out-and-back diversion to see St John's Well. On return, we go left, then right, to St John's Church along Daggett Lane.

After looking inside the church, we come out and take the p.r.o.w. running along the north side of the churchyard. At the end of the churchyard we turn left and at the next wall corner, strike diagonally right over the hummocky ground of old earthworks. Noting Drummer's Well to our right, we pass through a gate, then over a footbridge and from here we can just

Church Wood

Lowthorpe

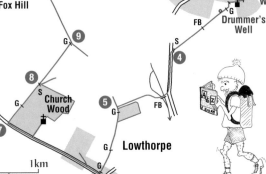

0   1km
0   0.5 mile

From there the path follows the outside of the plantation to the route intersection at (5). We turn left for 40m and go through the gate on our right. Taking care not to stray too far over to the right, we head across the field to the waymarked plank bridge and then over one more field to the road in Lowthorpe (6).

A right turn takes us past Lowthorpe Lodge and on to the drive leading to St Martin's Church which is certainly worth visiting. When we leave the church, we continue on the road and turn right at the signed footpath (7).

At (8) where the p.r.o.w. splits into two, we stay on the left branch and continue along the fieldside to the junction at (9). Here we go left to Bracey Bridge (10) where short walkers take the bus or parked cars back to the start.

The longer walk *crosses carefully* over the A614, goes down the banking and follows the left-hand edge of the trees in Quintin Bottom – the reason for coming on this walk.

The way is clear but after the second field boundary we avoid the tendency to stay too close to the trees and instead aim for the gap in the next boundary slightly over to our left. Then from there we head for the field corner boundary where it intersects with the line of power cables (11). After this the hedge gaps are clearly waymarked into Kilham.

At (12) the p.r.o.w. splits; we fork left across the field, go through the gate and along the path, turn right on the pebble drive, pass through the back of the pub and emerge opposite All Saints Church.

To see the church we turn left on the road and use the path access on our right. When we leave, we use the steps at the other end of the churchyard and continue along East Street.

At the far end of the village pond (13), we go right. The road soon becomes a track and, after going through a gate, we stay by the beck for 100m before turning sharp left, then right over the footbridge. The path soon curves left and, almost immediately, we take the gap in the hedge on our right. Bearing left, we walk along the fieldside and past the turkey farm to Harpham Lane (14).

We go right, left, then at the next right corner, we leave the tarmac and go straight ahead on the track called Green Lane. Some 50m on our right is the path that will take us across the fields towards Burton Agnes.

Gates, stiles and breaks in the hedges give our direction and after three fields we spot Burton Agnes Church and aim just to its right.

Crossing Sandy Lane (15) we continue in the same direction over two more fields before the path bends left (16), takes us down under more electricity cables and then comes up to Rudston Road (17). Turning right, we walk down to the A614, turn left and return with care to our start.

Special Interest – Walk Q

Burton Agnes 'fortified farmstead' of Agnes, wife of Adam who held the manor in the 12th century

Harpham unclear; possibly 'homestead where the harp was played'

Lowthorpe possibly 'Lagi's village'

Bracey Bridge 'Bried's ford' (later replaced by a bridge)

Kilham probably 'homestead at the kilns' (or springs)

Quintin Bottom is shown on the OS map as a woodland plantation along Lowthorpe Beck and is a clear reminder of the influence of the St Quintin family in this area. 'Bottom' usually refers to a dry vale in chalk country but in this case a stream flows on the floor of the shallow valley.

The **St Quintin family** were lords of the manor of Harpham from the late 12th until the 20th century and, although there is no trace remaining of the family house, their memorials in the village church ensure that they are not forgotten. The link between family and village still exists today.

Harpham is said to have been the birthplace in 640 AD of **St John of Beverley** and the village church is dedicated to him.

There are some remnants of a Norman church, but the building dates mainly from the 14th century and was constructed by Sir William St Quintin whose alabaster tomb, dated 1349, is inside the church.

The stained glass windows in the north chapel and east window make an extraordinary display. They show the shields of the St Quintin family from 1066 to 1795 and include 28 successive members. The windows were commissioned by the last baronet Sir William St Quintin who died in 1797. Other stone and brass memorials remind us of the influence of the family in Harpham's life.

The Drummer Boy's Well, surrounded by an iron railing, lies to the west of the church. Legend tells how Tom Hewson, the drummer boy, was accidentally knocked down the well by one St Quintin and drowned. From then on, whenever a St Quintin, Lord of Harpham, was about to die, the sound of Tom's drum beating at the bottom of the well could be heard.

St John's Well is dedicated to St John of Beverley but may be pre-Christian in origin. St John founded, and was buried in, Beverley Minster where his tomb became an important medieval pilgrimage shrine. Many miracles were attributed to the Saint and Harpham village also became a place of pilgrimage with people travelling from all over the country to the Holy Well. St John is known as the patron saint of the deaf and the dumb.

St Martin's Church, Lowthorpe dates from the 1300s but is thought to be the successor of an Anglo-Saxon church which once stood on the site. The remains of an Anglo-Saxon cross, found in the graveyard in 1932, are displayed inside the building. Also of interest is the 'Plague Cross' on the outside of the east wall. This is traditionally thought to have been the market cross from Kilham.

Kilham's former prosperity is indicated by some of its attractive 18th century houses but the village suffered as competition grew from Driffield. This decline started long before the cutting of the Driffield Canal in 1770. Kilham had the distinction of housing the Pigeon Corps during the Second World War.

All Saints Church is another post-Conquest church with Norman nave, font and a particularly fine south doorway. As with other churches in the region, it stands on a prominent mound which is likely to have been the site of an earlier pagan worship centre.

Burton Agnes Hall is regarded as one of nation's best country houses. Since the 1170s the estate has never been sold but has passed by marriage through successive generations. The Hall, with its fine collection of paintings, and the Gardens, which won the Historic Houses Garden of the Year Award in 2005, are open to the public from spring to autumn.

St Martin's Church, Burton Agnes lies at the end of a superb avenue of ancient yew trees. The original wooden church was rebuilt in the 12th century and parts of the Norman nave walls and restored chancel arch remain. As might be expected in an estate village there are numerous memorials to the family living at the adjacent Hall. Robert Wilberforce, son of the anti-slavery campaigner, was rector from 1840-45 and he was responsible for rescuing the Norman font from the garden where it had been serving as a flower bowl.

Close by the church is the Norman Manor House with its rare undercroft.

Special Interest – Walk R

Riplingham either 'home of Rippel and his people' or 'homestead of those living near the strip of woodland'

Rowley 'rough hill'

Brantingham 'homestead of the Brantings (those dwelling on steep slopes)'

Brantingham Thorpe outlying hamlet ('thorpe') belonging to Brantingham

Hunsley possibly 'Hund's clearing' or 'clearing belonging to the Hundred'

Ellerker 'alder marsh'

Riplingham, Rowley, Weedley and Wauldby form a group of four deserted villages in this area.

Riplingham has never been totally abandoned. The site was excavated in the 1950s. As well as investigating a prehistoric double dyke, archaeologists unearthed a well-made road, probably of late 18th century date, and house sites. One of the houses had been completely ruined by the late 14th century but there was renewed building activity around 1500 at the western end of the village. Some time after the 1801 Enclosure Act, there were about a dozen houses still standing near the crossroads. Today earthworks can easily be seen marking the sites of former houses and boundaries.

Rowley with its fine church and hotel called Rowley Manor is an attractive venue for weddings. The hotel, dating from 1710, was originally built as a rectory. However, apart from these buildings and the rectory farmhouse, the settlement lacks other buildings and there is no trace of a village site.

St Peter's Church is a large building but without a local congregation. Religious persecution may be said to have been a factor aiding the vacation of the village. Before he died in 1625 King James I had decreed that the **Book of Sports** should be read in churches throughout the land. The book instructed church-goers to take part in dancing, archery and games each week after Sunday worship. The Reverend Ezekiel Rogers, a prominent East Yorkshire Puritan, refused to obey the royal edict and, rather than compromise his beliefs, opted to leave England and establish a new settlement in North America. It used to be thought that this had led to the depopulation of the village but it is now known that most of the 20 families that sailed with Reverend Rogers in 1638 came from elsewhere in the East Riding and some from even further afield. Today the people of Rowley, Massachusetts, number several thousand and have maintained the link with Rowley, Yorkshire. In 1994 the New England congregation presented St Peter's Church with the 'Ezekiel Rogers Window' in memory of their founding father. Visitors from the United States record their pilgrimages in the Church Visitors' Book.

Brantingham is an estate village with many of the buildings constructed from the local Jurassic limestone. The large war memorial, however, was built using fragments from the old Hull Town Hall which was demolished in 1912. Around the village on the tops of gateposts are ornamental urns salvaged from the same source.

All Saints Church was rebuilt in 1872 but retains some parts, including the font, that appear to be from the earlier Norman Church and the list of priests goes back to 1238. Unusual features include a sliding communion rail and oak 'gravestones'.

Brantinghamthorpe Hall (not to be confused with Brantingham Hall) lies in private parkland to the SE of the village. For a time it was the home of Christopher Sykes, brother of Sir Tatton Sykes II. Christopher was MP for East Yorkshire and his Private Members Bill to prevent the shooting of wild seabirds earned him the nickname of 'the Seagulls' Friend'.

WALK R
Riplingham and Rowley

Map: Explorer 293
S.E.P.: Brantingham Village Hall (940294)
Bus: 155 from Hull
Longer walk (incl Rowley): 10.8 miles
Shorter walk (incl Rowley): 9.4 miles
Special interest:
Lost villages

Riplingham Lost Village site

The **R** Walk focuses on the lost medieval village of Riplingham, with a possible extension to the neighbouring Rowley. The suggested start is from the village hall in Brantingham (1) so that there is a section of the Wolds Way at both the beginning and the end of the circuit. A quick look at the southern part of the village can precede the main walk.

We walk NE through Brantingham and at the village green fork left past the pond. Turning right at the T-junction, we pass the impressive Brantingham Hall and at the next junction bend left, past attractive limestone cottages, up Dale Road. This is the first of four dales we shall see on this walk.

All Saints Church, standing well beyond the village, is on our right as we continue up the lane to the sharp right bend at (2). Here we turn off left at the gate, following the Wolds Way as it climbs gently up a side valley. Where the track splits into track and path, we use the path to the right, going between the two fences, up to the gate at the top of the rise.

We descend fairly steeply, turn right before Woodale Farm, swing right again and, staying on the Wolds Way, quickly bear left at the gate as we leave the main track in Woo Dale.

We go down, then rise steeply up the opposite side of the valley and go through a gate. Soon the path bends left at another gate and levels off. We are directed right-left through the belt of trees just

before Mount Airy Farm and then at the path junction (3) we leave the Wolds Way and go right.

Soon we turn left on the wide track and spot ahead to our right a row of green aircraft sheds that use the long field as an airstrip.

We turn right behind the sheds and follow the belt of trees as we cross Cave Wold (perspiring, perhaps, up Sweatty Hill?). A trig point marks the highest point on Great Wold before we come to Riplingham Road at (4).

Turning right and then bearing left at the next fork (5), we come to the site of medieval Riplingham. There is plenty of evidence in the form of mounds and embankments to indicate the extent of the former village but we need to use the gaps in the hedge to see properly. Riplingham House, by contrast, remains a sturdy and imposing dwelling.

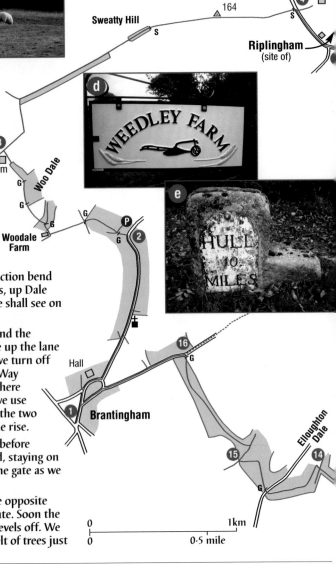

After going straight over the crossroads at (6) we continue to the junction at (7). If we fork left and then take the path at (8), we can view Rowley Church and

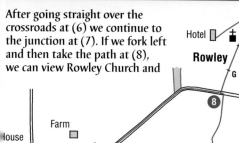

Rowley Manor before returning across the fields to the road at (9). However, the p.r.o.w. access to the church is awkward and involves a duplication of route which we may not think is worth the effort. So if we omit this visit, we fork right at (7) and stay on the busy Hull road to (9).

Shortly after (9) we turn right off the road and take the Beverley 20 tarred track leading to York Grounds Farm. This farm has been worked on organic principles since 1949.

Bending right at the farm sheds and silos, we are led on to the path crossing at Turtle Hill (10) and here the shorter walk turns right. The longer route carries straight on to Wauldby Manor Farm and here, still on the Wolds Way, we turn left-right and continue to the T-junction at the end of the field (11).

Ignoring the enticements of Great Gutter Lane, we turn right on the path going parallel to the concrete drive, pass the old mausoleum in the trees on our left, and join the road at (12).

A left turn leads us to the sharp bend about 400m further on (13) and now we turn right into the trees following the High Hunsley Circuit. After the track bends right, the route is still tree-lined on both sides.

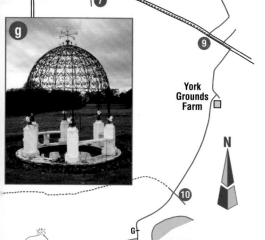

Wauldby Manor Farm

Mausoleum

About 40m after the path crossing at (14) our path swings left and leads us down to the road in the bottom of Elloughton Dale.

Going through the gate offset to our left on the opposite side of the road, we continue between the trees and up the side of another dale to the path junction at (15). Here we turn *right* (the direction says to Brantingham) and go for 100m before being directed left.

We now have an easy stroll, with good views of the Humber estuary, to the gate at (16). A final left turn takes us down the steep face of the chalk scarp and into Brantingham.

WALK S
Sigglesthorne

Map: Explorer 295
S.E.P.T.: Hornsea car park (198473)
                 or in Sigglesthorne or Seaton villages
Buses: 240, 246 Hull-Hornsea
Longer walk distance: **9.3 miles**
Shorter walk
                 (excl Hornsea Town Trail):   **7.7 miles**
Special interest:
                 Hornsea Mere, Wassand Hall

Hornsea Mere

There is room for three cars opposite to St Lawrence Church in Sigglesthorne (1) and the route description begins from there.

We go northwards through Sigglesthorne to the B1244 road (2), turn right and walk on the pavement into Seaton. The road twists left and right in the village and immediately after the Swan Inn we turn left down the side road to Bewholme.

Turning right at the crossing (still on Bewholme Lane), we continue to the left bend in the road and here leave the tarmac at the indicated stile (3).

From here the p.r.o.w. crosses diagonally to the footbridge in the field far corner and then follows field edges for the next 1.3 miles. The path is slightly offset to the left at Mill Lane and does a left-right twist later on but navigation is no difficulty as we make our way to Seaton Road (4).

We turn left and use the pavement alongside the B1244 to bring us to the edge of Hornsea. At (5), just after the white-painted house called The Pillars, we fork right down Back Westgate. From here we start to look for features of special interest on the **Town Trail**.

We soon come to the T-junction at Scalby Place, turn left to Market Place, go right to the traffic lights and turn left by St Nicholas Church into Newbegin, the main shopping thoroughfare. (Those omitting the Town Trail go on down Southgate.)

On Newbegin we must see the old farmhouse that is now the Hornsea Folk Museum and, next to it, the Hornsea Pottery Collection.

At Willows Drive (6) we take a look at Bettison's Folly along to our right and then return and cross the car park to enter Hall Garth Park. This is a delightful green space in the centre of the town. We bear right over the grass and make for the skate board area at the far corner of the park. Just to the right (7) are the iron gates leading us out of the park on to Cliff Road ... we read how our names have all been individually recorded here!

We turn left as far as Eastgate and then go right to the sea-front (8) where we turn right again and have the choice (if the tide is out) of walking either on the sand or the promenade.

Noting the considerable facelift of the promenade, we continue to the iconic Trans-Pennine Trail beacon at (9). A right turn inland takes us to the old railway station. Here the Town Trail bends right on Railway Street before turning left at the

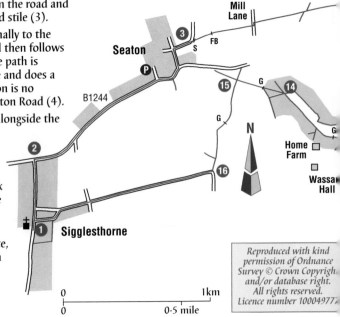

Mill Lane

Seaton

B1244

Home Farm

Wassar Hall

N

Sigglesthorne

0   1km
0   0.5 mile

Memorial Gardens and finishing in the town centre. The long walk bears left on to the old railway that forms the Trans-Pennine Trail.

Continuing for a little over half a mile we reach the roundabout at the 5-way road intersection at (10). We go straight over and carry on down Marlborough Avenue. At the end of this road we are directed right and take the bridleway across the allotments. This path brings us to Hull Road (11).

Crossing the road, and turning left, we soon come to the signposted footpath on our right (12). Here we leave the road and go over the grassy area known as Cherry Garths. Over to our left, beyond the high embankment, lies the site of the former medieval village of Southorpe. To our right, is Hornsea Mere.

Following the field edge, we pass the intriguingly named Snipe Ground and soon leave the hedge line to cross diagonally over three small fields to the double gate at (13).

We go right at the gates and take the broad track leading to Wassand Hall but we bypass the Hall, staying on the tree-lined tarmac bridleway to the path turning off left at (14). This takes us over rough ground to a small gate from where we continue to the sunken track at (15).

We turn left on this track for about 650m to the road corner at (16) and here go right along Wassand Balk back to Sigglesthorne. We cross Great Hatfield Road, fork left up Church Lane and left again back to St Lawrence Church.

HORNSEA

Hall Garth Park

B1244

Hornsea Mere

Snipe Ground

Southorpe (site of)

Trans Pennine Trail

Special Interest – Walk S

Sigglesthorne 'Sigel's thorn tree'

Seaton 'farmstead near the lake'

Hornsea probably 'lake in which lies a projecting piece of land'

Wassand 'sand bank or sandy shore near the ford'

Sigglesthorne is recorded in the Domesday Survey (1086) as having a priest and church belonging to St John of Beverley. The present church of **St Lawrence** is not the same one, though it dates from the 12th century and probably occupies the same site. However, there have been numerous alterations and additions in a variety of building materials so that little of the Norman church remains.

It is thought that the weight of the tower is so great that it may been been responsible for the tilting of the church towards the south.

In the churchyard is a long stone slab. This is believed to have been a medieval altar but at the Reformation it was taken from the church and used as a footbridge across a local stream. It was later retrieved and used a a gravestone.

Wassand Hall is a fine Regency House and its estate has been in the hands of one family since 1520. Hornsea Mere is part of the estate and the house,

gardens and parks are open to the public on selected days. The recently restored walled gardens were probably first established in the 16th century.

Hornsea Mere is Yorkshire's largest natural lake. It is the last of the once numerous meres that lay in the hollows of the undulating boulder clay of Holderness. The hamlets of Hornsea Burton and Hornsea Beck have been lost to the sea and the present town of Hornsea developed from a village lying beside the mere.

In the 19th century **Hornsea** attempted to develop its potential as a seaside resort attracting both day-trippers and residents from nearby Hull. However, the ideas for

Quaker Cottage was given to The Society of Friends (Quakers) by Peter Acklam in 1750. It was used as a meeting house and the garden as a burial ground until 1819. The property still belongs to The Society of Friends.

creating a whole new town were never implemented and the failure of the pier was a serious setback. It was opened in 1880, partially destroyed in the same year and then dismantled in 1897.

Hornsea Museum is the East Riding's best independent museum and well worth a visit. There is an extensive collection of folk life exhibits in a former farm house that was occupied by the Burns family for 300 years. In adjoining cottages is a display of over 2,000 pieces of Hornsea Pottery, recognised as the national collection. The museum is open from spring to autumn.

St Nicholas Church contains in the churchyard a restored medieval cross which formerly stood in the Market Place.

Town Trail In 2004 Hornsea residents devised a 'Curiosity Trail' around the town to draw attention to features of special interest. These are identified by numbered markers and some of these are included in the photo treasure hunt for this walk. And where do you find the cryptic message: 'Enter ... with title free – You'll find your name is wrought on me'?

WALK T
Thorngumbald

Maps: Explorer 292 and 293
S.E.P.: Church Lane, Thorngumbald (207263)
Buses: 75, 76, 77 from Hull
Longer walk distance: **11.7 miles**
Shorter walk (using bus for return): **7.8 miles**
        (Note: buses run regularly Hedon-Thorn)
Special interest:
        Hedon Town Trail

Probably the best time of year to do this walk is late May when the hawthorn blossoms are in full flower – throughout the walk we are reminded how beautiful the hedgerows appear in late spring.

The start is from the car park at the shops on Church Lane in Thorngumbald (1). From the car park we turn right, go through the housing estate to the road crossing at (2) and turn right in the direction of Paull.

Shortly after Green Marsh Farm, we turn right at the fingerpost and footbridge (3).

A fieldside path takes us beside Haylands Drain to the path leading to Villa Farm (4). Here we cross to our right and immediately turn left to follow the wider, deeper Thorngumbald Drain. We may see swans in the drain and hear the chirruping of agitated warblers in the rushes competing with the skylarks above the fields as we make our way to Thorngumbald Road (5).

Crossing over, we take the track offset slightly to our left past the gas storage installations.

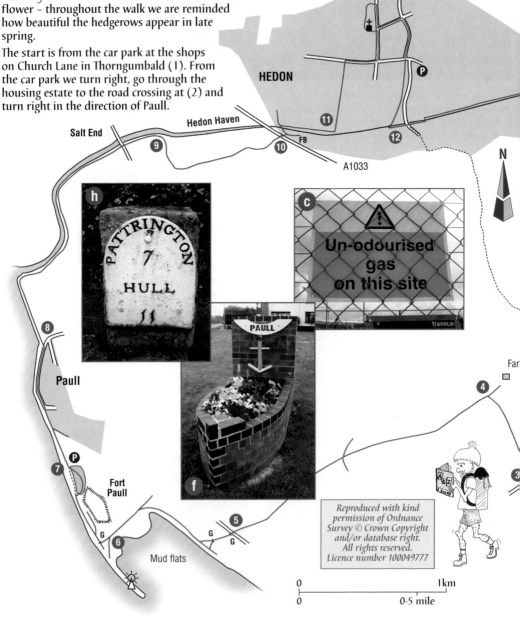

HEDON

Hedon Haven

Salt End

9

10

FB

11

12

A1033

N

h

PATTRINGTON
7
HULL
11

c

Un-odourised
gas
on this site

Transco

8

PAULL

Paull

Far

4

7

P

Fort
Paull

f

3

5

G

G

G

Mud flats

6

Reproduced with kind permission of Ordnance Survey © Crown Copyright and/or database right. All rights reserved. Licence number 100049777

0   1km
0   0·5 mile

Where the path divides, we bear right up on to the embankment and continue around the area of tidal mudflats.

At (6) we bend right and, walking beside the Humber Estuary, go past the barely visible installations of Fort Paull. At the information pillar we can turn right into Paull Woodland and swing round left to the car park (7) before continuing along the path into Paull. Entering the settlement, we note the damage done by sea erosion to the coastal defences.

We walk through the village along Main Street and at the end of the houses (8) leave the road and bear left up to

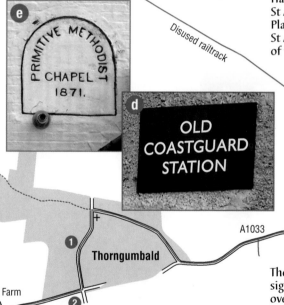

the embankment again. We are now on the Salt End tidal defences. These were opened in 1998 with 'armourstone' (boulders) on the seaward side and a variety of colourful wild flowers growing on the grassy landward side.

Staying along the side of the estuary, we carry on for about 450m before swinging right following the tidal channel of Hedon Haven. We cross Paull Road and stay by the channel to the waymarker at (9). Here the man-made waterway forks left but

we bend right and follow the line of the original channel.

At the A1033 Hedon bypass (10) we go under the road, turn left on the footbridge over the Haven, continue for 40m and then turn right to walk on the greenway beside the Burstwick Drain.

Just after passing a small skate-board area, and opposite a narrow footbridge over the Drain, we come to a wide grass corridor (11) leading into Hedon. Here we turn left.

We follow the green corridor to New Road, cross over and turn right, go past the Methodist Church and come to St Augustine's Gate. Before turning left here, we should take a look at New Hall just ahead on the right on Fletcher Gate. St Augustine's Gate then brings us up to Market Place where we bear left into Church Gate for St Augustine's Church and Market Hill, the site of the original market.

We bend right to go past Hedon Nursery School, right down Wayfbain and right yet again down Soutter Gate. At the crossroads we go left along Magdalen Gate.

Turning first right into Baxter Gate, we take a peep at the Kilnsea Cross in the gardens of Holyrood House down the first drive on our right. Then we continue down Baxter Gate to the T-junction with Fletcher Gate. Here short walkers either catch a bus or retrieve their cars from the car park and return to Thorngumbald.

The long walk goes across the road to follow the signed bridleway. This takes us to a footbridge over Burstwick Drain (12). Crossing the Drain, we turn left to Thorn Road, go straight over and now follow the wide ditch for another mile. We walk first on the right of the water, then on the left, and at the end of the houses bend right to the disused rail track at (13).

Bending right, we follow the former rail line for 1.4 miles to Station Road (14). Here we turn right along the pavement to the A1033 and then right again into Thorngumbald. Thankfully the pavement continues all the way to St Mary's Church where we turn left back to our start.

Special Interest – Walk T

Thorngumbald's original name was 'Thorn' but the de Gumbaud family were lords of the manor and added their family name to 'Thorn' in the 13th century to distinguish it from other 'Thorns'.

Hedon probably 'uncultivated land' plus 'on' (not 'high hill' because it is not on a hill)

Paull not clear. Perhaps refers to a 'stake or boundary pole marker'

Thorngumbald used to be a hamlet within the medieval parish of Paull and remained small until the 20th century. **St Mary's Church** looks relatively modern but parts of the building date back to medieval times and there are two doorways thought to be from about 1200. The font is Norman and the vestry on the south side dates from the 1700s.

Paull has had a fort since the 1500s. Its slightly raised position above the Humber was a useful strategic advantage. With the threat of invasion by Napoleon, the fort was rebuilt in 1807 and then later extensively reconstructed between 1861-64. In the 20th century it acted as an anti-aircraft battery against German bombers in World War II.

The former lighthouse that we pass on our walk is now a private home and was built in 1836 but replaced in 1870 by the two towers to the south-east. These stand on the spit of land at Cherry Cobb Sands Bank. This area has seen an interesting example of one way in which sea defences can be improved to help reduce the effects of coastal flooding. The policy is called

'managed realignment' and involves building a new line of defence further inland from the old one. The original defences are then breached and the tide allowed to flow in and out of the newly created area of mudflats instead of attacking and flooding inhabited land. At the same time as improving sea defences, 'managed realignment' can enhance local ecosystems because inter-tidal mudflats and the salt marsh which develops on them provide an important food source for wading birds and other wildfowl. The Paull Holme project has attracted black tailed godwits and even avocets.

Hedon is a town that deserves far more acclaim than it normally receives. It is a classic example of a medieval '**New Town**' and was founded by William le Gros ('the Fat One') in about 1130 as a port with access to the Humber via **Hedon**

Haven. King Stephen (1135-1154) ordered a royal mint to be set up and the town's first proven Charter, given by Henry II in 1158, gave the burgesses of Hedon privileges equal to those enjoyed by the citizens of York and Lincoln.

Numerous other **Royal Charters** followed and in 2000 the town celebrated the 800th anniversary of the Charter granted in 1200 by King John. In 1348 Hedon was the first town in Yorkshire to be

limited by the development of Ravenser Odd and Hull as well as the silting of Hedon Haven.

Hedon's first Mayor took office in 1348 and he was protected in his duties by the Sergeant-at-Mace who would carry his mace to defend the Mayor. Gradually the mace became more elaborate, being clad in silver, but it remained an effective weapon. Hedon is the proud possessor of the oldest **civic mace** in the country. It was given to the town in 1415.

Much later, to celebrate his election to Parliament in 1669, Henry Guy presented a silver Great Mace to the borough. Guy was also responsible for building the Town Hall in 1692. His portrait hangs in the council chamber together with a painting of William Pulteney who was MP for Hedon in 1705. He became Earl of Bath and holds the honour of having been Prime Minister for just one day. Located behind the Town Hall is Hedon Museum – its website details the opening times.

At Holyrood House in Baxtergate is found the **Kilnsea Cross**. The Cross is said to have been first erected at Ravenser where Henry Bolingbroke landed in 1399 to overthrow Richard II and make himself King Henry IV.

St Augustine's Church is the

given a Charter of Incorporation by Edward III, allowing the right to elect a Mayor, Bailiffs and other local officers. Further Charters gave permission for Hedon to hold regular markets and fairs.

In 1295 Hedon returned two members of Parliament and, although the borough was not represented in Parliament for many years, from 1547 until the Great Reform Act of 1832 the town was permanently represented. Yet despite these apparent advantages, Hedon 's growth was

WAYFBAIN
WAYPAYNE LANE - FINKLE STREET

only one of the town's three medieval churches to survive and it is a reminder of Hedon's past importance. Dating from the early 13th century, it is one of the five biggest parish churches in the county.

FOUNDED BY
George Painter
1562

WALK U
Uncleby

Map: Explorer 294
S.E.P.:   Kirby Underdale village hall by kind
        permission of Halifax Estates
        (806586)
Bus: No bus service

Longer walk distance:	9.7 miles
Medium walk (by Beck Plantation):	7.1 miles
Shorter walk (by Baffham):	5.2 miles

As with Painsthorpe, the actual settlement of Uncleby has only a couple of buildings but the OS map also names Uncleby Beck, Wold, Hill, Top and Barn, so there should be no doubt where we are.

We leave Kirby Underdale village hall (1) to go WNW down to the gate in the field corner and then follow the field edges, over one stile, to a second stile at (2). Following the waymark, we turn right, then bend left by the hedge and continue to the farm drive for Glebe Farm (3). Here the short walk turns right; the long walk crosses the drive and carries on beside a ditch until we pass through a hedge and re-join the road at (4).

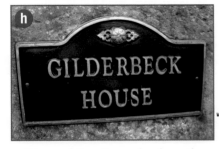

We now follow the road as far as the drive to Primrose Hill Farm (5). The medium distance walk carries on for some 400m before turning off right but the long walk turns left up the farm drive.

Just before the farm, we use the gate on our right, turn left and carry on down the field to the wide ditch at (6). Here we turn right.

The p.r.o.w. carries on through two gates and at the following field corner we cross a footbridge and go left. At the next boundary we turn sharp right and continue through three gates to emerge on Barf Lane (7). Here a right turn takes us into Bugthorpe.

Turning right in Bugthorpe, we can visit the Church before continuing on the main street and, about 100m past the end of the churchyard, turning left down the first side road (8). The path at the end of the road squeezes between hedge and fence, crosses the old moat and goes over the footbridge at Bugthorpe Beck.

From here the route has been diverted. We bear right for some 35m, go through the gap in the hedge and stay by the beck to the gate at (9). Turning 90° left through the kissing-gate and, staying on the right side of the hedge, we continue up the gentle slope.

At the top we turn right. Soon we leave the main track, turning left and following

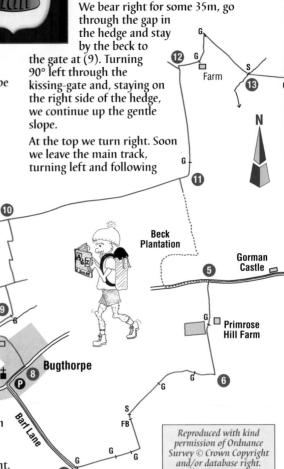

field edges, with a couple of right-left shimmies, to go through the hedge gap on our right at (10).

We now follow the county boundary for 0.8 mile to the turning at (11). Here we have to go left up the slope to the path junction at (12) where we go right, with the hedge on our right, to Gilderbeck House.

At this point we bear left on the tarred lane for some 150m before turning off right, through the wide gate and over the ditch. We follow the tractor trail, keeping the fence over to our right and avoiding the gap in the hedge that soon appears on our left, before bending slightly right to the stile at Gilder Beck (13).

The path turns up left and we stay at the fieldside, pass through a small gate, and come to the field corner at (14). At this point the short walk joins in; the long walk turns left through the gate and swings right alongside the trees.

At the end of the wood we carry on to the minor road and turn right for 100m to the gate at (15). We do not go through the gate but turn left with the fence on our right. After the next small gate, the sheep track-path bends slightly left to yet another gate, then gently right, past a badger sett, to the hedge corner. From here we follow the hedge to the gate at (16). In front of us lies Open Dale.

We turn right and, crossing rather damp ground, come to the confluence of Opendale Beck and another small stream. The path has been diverted, so we take the gate on our right to a second gate, cross the culverted stream and go over the field to the fence at (17).

Our route now turns left up the scarp face of the Wolds. We pass through three gates and make two left-right manoeuvres as we climb the hill to the road at (18). Turning right, we follow the road to the crossing at (19) and here go right again down Uncleby Hill.

Some 60m after the buildings that comprise Uncleby, we take the stile on our left (20). Crossing the field at 1.00 o'clock direction, we aim for the gate in the hedge facing us and go over another low rise to the footbridge over Uncleby Beck. From here we have a third spur to cross and then we come down to Kirby Beck and All Saints Church. A right turn on the road takes us back to the village hall.

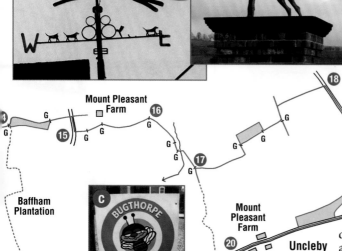

0 ———— 1km
0 ———— 0·5 mile

WALK V
Vale of York

Map: Explorer 291
S.E.P.: Howden car park (749281)
Bus: 155 Hull-Goole
Longer walk distance: 10.1 miles
Shorter walk alternative: 5.6 miles
Special interest:
      Howden Town Trail,
      Willow Tree plantations

This walk in the Vale of York focuses on the old market town of Howden and a variety of different length routes is possible. They all start in Howden and included with these notes are details of a short town trail that can be completed at the end of the main walk.

Leaving the pay-and-display car park (1) by the Bishop's Manor House, we turn right on to Hailgate and then fork left at the Y-junction to go in the direction of the M62. We cross the A614 and, using the pavement, continue along Broad Lane and over the M62 to the road junction for Kilpin (2).

Almost opposite the road turn-off, we cross the footbridge, turn immediately left and walk by the field edge. Following Howden 20 waymarks, we veer left through some trees, stay by the ditch and cross diagonally over a factory access road.

Soon we go through a gate and bear left again before swinging right to avoid going into Howdendyke. It's not long before we come to the River Ouse where we continue along the embankment on the Trans-Pennine Trail (3). We now have a little under three miles of easy riverside walking.

We pass beneath the noisy M62 motorway, under the Boothferry swingbridge, left of the riverbank cottages and come to the gate at (4). Here the shorter walk turns right to Knedlington; the longer walk continues ahead.

The path temporarily leaves the river bank and we lose sight of the Ouse as it flows on the other side of the scrubby woodland of Asselby Island. This means we miss a clear view of the River Aire joining with the Ouse. Shortly after

the path meets the river again, and with Drax power station ahead of us, we leave the Trans-Pennine Trail and turn right to Asselby on the byway called Landing Lane (5).

At the main road in Asselby (6) we turn left and walk through the village. Near the end of the houses, the road Z-bends right and left. At the left bend (7) we turn right and 40m later go left over the stile on to the p.r.o.w.

We follow the fieldside path over a couple more stiles and a plank bridge and then, after crossing one more field, bend right across the former Newsholme Marsh. Soon after the next stile we turn

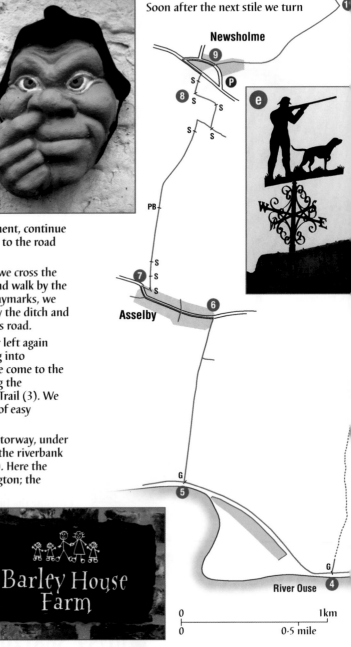

Newsholme

Asselby

Barley House Farm

River Ouse

0   1km
0   0·5 mile

right and then, walking round three sides of a square, go left, and left again to the stile at (8). A last right turn here will bring us to the A63.

Crossing the road, we go left, turn back right at the road sign for Newsholme and walk to Beech Tree Farm (9). Here we leave the tarmac, branching off left through the gate on to the wide track next to the farm.

For the next stretch of the walk we pass over very unusual farmland because here the main crop is willow trees. The p.r.o.w. runs in a general NE direction on a broad grassy strip to the T-junction at (10). Here there are **two** transverse grass strips; we take the farther one and turn 90° left, then quickly right. We walk on the right of the blackberry 'hedge' and follow the waymarks to (11). From here we turn right for 100m, left at the dyke for 115m and right again for about 175m to join the track at (12). Bearing left, we come to the railway crossing at (13). We have now re-joined the Howden 20 route.

We do not cross the rail line, or use the gate to our right, but turn back sharp right to follow the right-hand side of the hedge to the footbridge at the edge of the wood (14). Over the ditch, we jiggle right-left and follow the path on the right of the trees.

At the end of the wood where the path divides, we veer slightly left and a clear route leads us over the farmland of Howden Parks as we head towards Howden Minster. At Duck Swang Drain (15) (what a gorgeous name for a ditch) we go right for a short distance before turning left at the next wide track.

At the footbridge (16) we go right over another dyke and cross an open area to the A63 Selby Road (17). A left turn takes us back into Howden and, staying on the main road, we bend right, twist left into Northolmby Street and reach Pinfold Street. The Minster Church lies just to our right and this forms the start of the Town Trail.

Special Interest – Walk V

Howden 'valley by the spit of land' ('valley' is a reference to the *old* course of the Derwent)

Boothferry 'ferry of the Botheby family'

Knedlington 'farmstead of Cneddel and his people'

Asselby 'Askell's farmstead'

Newsholme 'the new houses' ('new' in 1086)

The **Vale of York** is the low and almost flat area of land lying west of the line of low Jurassic Hills

From the confluence of the Derwent with the Ouse, eastwards along the Humber, is a band of reclaimed salt marsh and to the north of this were large tracts of waterlogged carr land such as Wallingfen. This land was enclosed in the 1770s and drained by the Market Weighton Canal.

Willow Trees have been grown since 2000 by

Strawsons Energy Company for use as a 'green' fuel at Drax Power Station. The 'Willow Short Rotation Coppice' (SRC) is grown in plantations and

the 'crop' is harvested every three years. New shoots then grow up from the coppiced stumps. When first cut, the willow is over 50% moisture so it is wind-dried for three months to reduce the moisture content to about 30% before being sold to Drax.

Strawsons claim a number of advantages for 'Koolfuel', the product they make from Willow SRC. It is a renewable fuel; it is carbon neutral; it produces less CO_2 gas than fossil fuels and its development is sustainable because hardly any chemicals are put into the soil.

Moreover, there are distinct advantages for wildlife. Early studies suggest that SRC plantations provide a better wildlife habitat than the arable fields they replace. At Newsholme six varieties of willow are grown, each with its own different shape, structure and growth characteristics so this provides greater diversity of habitat. The shelter given by the trees has increased the number of bird species and by leaving wide wild flower corridors, the number of plant species has also grown. In plantations across the country, over 135 types of invertebrate have been counted in the willow canopies and nearly as many living on or under the ground.

and stretching to the Pennines. We have already visited the Vale on Walks **E** and **I**. For thousands of years the Vale has suffered extensive flooding from the Rivers Ouse and Derwent and so the glacial deposits of this lowland are covered with a layer of fertile alluvium. Flooding along the rivers is still a problem, although the **Barmby Tidal Barrage** can now be closed to stop tidal water from the River Ouse entering the Derwent and making flooding even worse. The Barrage serves other purposes, too. A sufficient depth of water can be maintained in the Derwent for navigation but the river level can also be kept low enough to permit drainage from surrounding fields. A supply of fresh water is available for pumping to Hull and elsewhere.

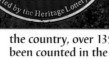

ALPHABETTING IN EAST YORKSHIRE

Howden was given to the Prince Bishops of Durham by William the Conqueror. It was the centre of a parish containing a dozen townships and was the focus of the Bishop's extensive Liberty of Howdenshire. This connection with Durham and the four annual fairs ensured the town's prosperity in early medieval days.

Howden's great prosperity came to an end in the 16th century. However, fortunes were revived in the 1700s when Howden became an important link in the network of national coaching services. Moreover, the growth of the famous Horse Fair, reputedly the largest in Europe and originating in 1200, led to the building of fine inns with their associated stabling facilities.

St Peter's Church (Howden Minster) dates from 1267 and replaced earlier Saxon and Norman churches. The eastern end of the building (the choir) suffered from neglect after the Reformation and the roof finally collapsed in 1696 and the roof of the chapter house in 1750. Today the western end of the medieval building survives as the parish church. Young visitors can search for the 30-odd 'Mousy Thompson' mice hidden around the building and a very helpful free information leaflet is available at the church.

Knedlington Old Hall, dating from the 17th century, is described by Pevsner & Neave as 'the finest small manor house in the East Riding' and so is worth viewing.

Boothferry Swing-bridge over the River Ouse was opened in 1929.

Howden Town Trail
The photographic Treasure Hunt trail around the centre of the town is designed to accompany part of the Civic Society's 'Walk through Howden's past'. The Society's trail follows a set of fine blue wall plaques which can be read at the same time as walkers look for the photo clues.

Facing the main west door of Howden Minster, we walk down Churchside to the Market Place. A right turn takes us on a tarred path into The Ashes playing fields.

We pass the remains of the Bishop's Manor House which is all that is left of the much bigger palace built by the Bishops of Durham who used Howden as a stopping point on their trips to London. Kings, in their turn, stayed here on visits north. The old course of the River Derwent flowed close to the site.

Our path turns right by the folly arch straddling the old moat that used to encircle an orchard and fishponds. Then at the left bend, we leave the path and go diagonally right across the grass to the far corner of the playing field. Going through the gate, we turn right on Treeton Road and walk to Pinfold Street.

Here we turn right back to the town centre, carry on past the Minster and continue ahead along Bridgegate until we reach Bishopgate.

A right turn leads us to Hailgate where we go right again and right once more along the snicket back to Market Place. A final left turn takes us to the Minster.

WALK W
Wetwang

Maps: Explorer 294 and 300
S.E.P.: Main Street, Wetwang (933591)
Bus: 135 from Driffield
Longer walk (incl Monument): **10.2 miles**
Shorter north loop (incl Monument): **7.5 miles**
Shorter south loop: **6.6 miles**
Special interest:
      Wetwang chariot burials,
      Long Distance Trackways

d

IN MEMORY OF
RICHARD WHITELEY
(O.B.E.)
HONORARY MAYOR OF WETWANG
1999 - 2005

This roughly square-shaped walk covers an area of exceptional archaeological importance. In addition to following sections of two ancient Green Lanes, we cross the site of the famous Iron Age chariot burials in the dry valley known as Wetwang-Garton Slack.

The start of the walk is from Main Street (1) (A166) in Wetwang where there is both bus access and room for roadside car parking. A visit to St Nicholas' Church is a good beginning and, on leaving the Church through the lych-gate, we turn right on Main Street, right again down Church Lane, bend left on Pulham Lane, go right at Southfield Road, first right again (still on Southfield Road) and walk to the fingerpost opposite Southfield Close (2). Here we go through the gap in the hedge on our left.

A well-worn path across the farmland touches two field corners, bends right along the hedge-side and joins Thorndale Lane (3). Turning left, we go for some 140m to the sharp bend in the road and now leave the tarmac to continue straight ahead on a wide grassy bridleway down the dry valley called Thorn Dale.

At the track junction (4) we turn left and continue along Tibthorpe Green Lane. With its high tree-lined sides and plentiful side-growth, this

forms an extremely attractive green corridor within the overall arable landscape. (Unlike the Sledmere Green Lane, this lane is not a ridgeway track and instead follows a much lower elevation.)

We cross straight over the B1248 road (5) and from here the lane is tarred until 100m before the next track crossing at (6). Turning left through the gap in the hedge, we follow the field edge up to the A166 at (7). Across the road, slightly to the right, the bridleway continues on the right of the hedge.

From here we start gently descending to the floor of Wetwang-Garton Slack. At the track marking the dismantled rail line (8), the shorter walk turns left towards Wetwang Grange and the longer route carries on ahead, dropping to the bottom of the slack. As we cross the floor of the shallow valley we should be aware that this is the location of the important prehistoric burial site.

a

IN THIS PLACE
WAS FOUND
THE WETWANG
IRON AGE
CHARIOT BURIAL

HOGG THE BUILDER
APRIL 2001

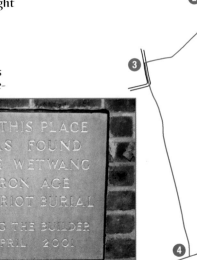

Rising gradually up the other side of the wide, shallow valley, we pass Garton Field Farm to our right, go over the farm track at the end of the trees (9) and continue up to the old ridgeway track of Sledmere Green Lane (10).

At this point, we should take the opportunity to see the ancient embankments hidden in the trees of Black Wood to our right. We only get glimpses of the structures through the vegetation but even so they still appear impressive. We may also wish to continue further along the Green Lane to look at the carvings on the Sir Tatton Sykes Monument.

Returning to the crossing at (10), we now have another couple of miles following the broad Sledmere Green Lane. We drop very gently down and have great views to the south and south-west across Wetwang Slack.

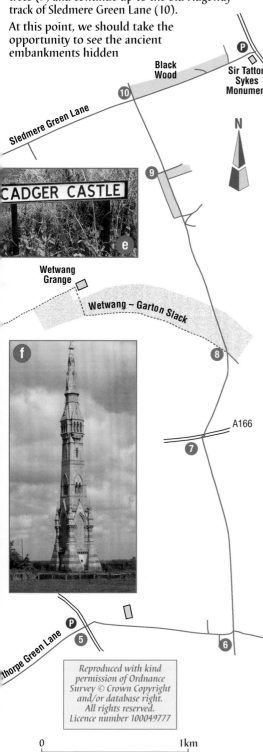

CADGER CASTLE

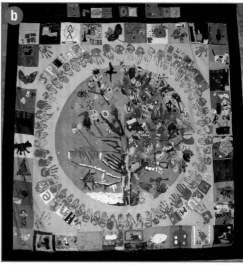

We cross the road to Sledmere (11) and stay on the Green Lane to the B1248 road at (12). Here it is possible to turn left and walk on the side verge to the stile and path at (13). However, the preferred route is to cross the road and continue for 150m to the fingerpost on the left. This directs us back over the cropped field to the B1248 and over the road to the path at (13).

We are now on the Chalkland Way and, aiming towards a black painted barn, we are led over one arable and one pasture field to go through the two gates at (14). Bearing right, we quickly join the A166 and turn left into Wetwang village.

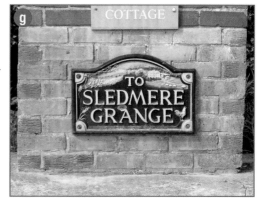

COTTAGE
TO SLEDMERE GRANGE

0   1 km
0   0·5 mile

Special Interest – Walk W

Wetwang 'field of summons for the trial of an action'

Wetwang-Garton Burial Site

On Walk **A** we crossed the site of the Arras Iron Age burial site, the first major prehistoric cemetery to be excavated on the Wolds.

During the 1980s and 1990s many more burial sites were investigated and the most important of these were in the gravel quarries of Wetwang-Garton Slack. Here, traces of an extensive prehistoric landscape were unearthed from the gravels in the bottom of the dry valley. Finds included Neolithic and Bronze Age barrows but also a large Iron Age cemetery. One writer describes how, from the air, the cluster of many square barrows made the cemetery look like a mass of frogspawn.

Sometimes the dead were buried with their weapons, along with pig remains, and they were always lying east to west. Others were found with pots or brooches, together with sheep remains, and they were usually laid north to south.

In six cases; three in Garton parish and three in Wetwang parish; the remains of dismantled carts or chariots were found and these graves also contained high-status objects suggesting the deceased had been wealthy leaders in the local Parisi tribe.

Then in 2001 newspapers reported the stunning find at the east end of Wetwang village of a 'fabulous' chariot burial to add to the list of those already discovered in the parish. This discovery was made during routine digging checks before new houses were built on the site. With the chariot were the remains of a crouched woman with her mirror and pieces of pig meat. The chariot had well-preserved metal bindings, inlaid coral decorations, sections of wheels and horse harnesses. This, say archaeologists, is proof that prehistoric Britons were not primitive. The chariot is thought to be very similar to the 4,000 carts that attempted to defend the Thames crossing against Caesar when he invaded 300 years later. In an elaborate reconstruction experiment, the BBC showed that such chariots were extremely serviceable vehicles.

Long Distance Trackways

A number of ancient trackways cross the Wolds. The two most important are the 'Towthorpe Ridgeway' running from Aldro to the North Sea coast and the 'Sledmere Green Lane' leading from Garrowby Hill to Rudston. These two prehistoric routes link up further west with the York and Escrick glacial moraines and so continue the routeways on drier ground across the marshy Vale of York.

The Sledmere Green Lane is a remarkable feature of the landscape because it has survived and been used in different ways for over 4,000 years. Archaeologists have identified the following different functions:

(a) It was used as a prehistoric trackway in the Bronze Age and maybe even earlier in Neolithic times.

(b) During the late Bronze Age systems of massive embankments were laid out on the Wolds as different tribal groupings attempted to define their territories (see Walk **H**). The Sledmere Green Lane was used as a boundary with a series of three parallel banks and ditches. On Walk **W** we see a well-preserved stretch in the trees of Black Wood.

(c) In late Iron Age times (around the first century BC) the land to the south of the Green Lane was divided up, enclosed and worked as small farm holdings. The ditches that separated the units led down the valley slope from the Green Lane. (We can imagine the scene as we look down the valley side around High Bitings.)

(d) Excavations at the embankments near the Sir Tatton Sykes Monument have revealed that during the Anglo-Saxon period one of the ditches was being used as a cemetery.

(e) In the medieval period sections of the Green Lane embankments were used as boundary lines to separate neighbouring townships. A 'township' was the area of land (similar in size to a present-day parish) surrounding a medieval village and supporting a self-sufficient farming community.

(f) Later still, the ancient trackway provided a convenient route, with some deviations, for an 18th century coach road.

(g) Today, walkers value the Green Lane's designation as a public right of way.

The **Sir Tatton Sykes Monument** was erected in 1865 to commemorate the fourth baronet of Sledmere who had the reputation of being generous towards the poor (but cruel to his children). It is said that a beggar would never leave his back door without a piece of bread and a pint of home-brewed ale. At his death in 1863, over 3,000 people attended his funeral.

Special Interest – Walk X

Bridlington very controversial; possibly 'Berhtel's farmstead'

Hilderthorpe 'Hildiger's village'

Wilsthorpe 'Wifel's village'

Bessingby 'Besing's farmstead'

The Chi Rho Symbol

When we were devising the Alphabet Walks, finding a location for the letter **X** proved, not surprisingly, a little difficult. However, we wanted to include Bridlington as one of East Yorkshire's major towns and so we hit on the idea of using the Chi Rho symbol in Bridlington Priory as the focus for the **X** Walk. This motif is a combination of the first two letters of the Greek word CHRISTOS (XPISTOS) or, in English, CHRIST. Chi Rho, that is, the **X** with the **P** superimposed, is the oldest monogram for Christ and was commonly used by the early Christians. The Chi Rho monogram is found above the High Altar at the east end of the Priory.

Bridlington's Augustinian Priory was based on the existing Church of St Mary and was at one time the richest Augustinian Priory in Yorkshire. John de Thwing was its most noted inhabitant and he joined the Priory as a canon in 1340 before becoming its Prior in 1363. During his life he was credited with many miracles, including raising the dead, and after he died in 1379 he was later canonised as St John of Bridlington, the last Englishman to be made a saint before the Reformation. The town became a centre of pilgrimage as pilgrims came from across the country to visit the holy man's shrine in the Priory Church.

When Henry VIII carried out his Dissolution of the English Monasteries in the late 1530s, Bridlington Priory suffered catastrophically. Most of the Priory buildings were demolished and only the nave of the church was left standing. This was because it acted as the parish church and this is the building we enter today.

On the outside north wall of the Priory is a cupboard-like recess that is thought may have been an oubliette. The Early Church is known to have sometimes imprisoned criminals in oubliettes where they starved to death. Yet some Christians volunteered for the ordeal, presumably believing that this form of self-torture would be rewarded in heaven.

St Mary's faces the same problems as all the nation's great churches: how does it stay open and alive for future generations whilst at the same time manage to pay its enormous maintenance bills?

Bridlington Priory by Dan Savage (inset photo above)

WALK X
X Marks The Spot

Map: Explorer 295
S.E.P.: Bridlington Market Place (172679)
Longer walk distance: 7.9 miles
Shorter walk alternative: 3.8 miles
Special interest:
Bridlington Priory and Town Trail

Walk **X** comprises several distinct elements and to see everything of interest may demand more than one visit to the town. The urban section of the walk combines an Old Town Trail with a Maritime Trail around the Harbour area. The full walk circuit extends along South Sands and returns via Bessingby.

Both walks commence at the Market Place car park (1) in Bridlington's Historic Old Town.

Leaving the car park by the Market Place entrance, we turn left, then left again to walk along High Street. Crossing over Scarborough Road we continue past the Bayle Museum on our right and approach Bridlington Priory.

Entry into this majestic building is essential for Alphabetters because the **X** symbol is to be found within the Church. Please do remember, however, that the Church is a House of Prayer and not a museum.

Once we have located our treasured **X** we leave the Priory by the west gate, turn back left on ourselves and follow the tarred path immediately next to the churchyard wall. We are led over a suburban road, along the side of the city cemetery and on to St Aidan Road (2). We turn right, then quickly

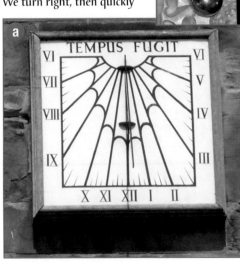

bend left at the Y-fork, veer left again at the roundabout and come to Queensgate Park.

Going diagonally right over the grass to the main road, we turn right, go under the rail bridge and continue on the road to Holy Trinity Church at (3). Taking the side road to the left of the church, we reach the seafront and here turn right along the coast.

The refurbished Beaconsfield Promenade merits a leisurely stroll, though when we reach the amusements we may prefer to walk on as quickly as possible! However, going around the edge of the harbour and past the Harbour Heritage Museum, we see ample evidence that Bridlington is still a working fishing port as well as a holiday destination. If time allows, we should make the effort to visit the nearby Beside the Seaside Museum on Bridge Street and from here the short walk returns through the town to the Market Place.

On the south side of the harbour, long walkers have the choice of walking on the sand or on the promenade (but treasure clue hunters would be advised to follow the latter). We pass the site of the medieval village of Hilderthorpe and stride on to the narrow access road at (4) - just before the site of another deserted settlement at Wilsthorpe.

Here we turn inland and follow the lane to the tarred bridleway at (5) where we turn right. At the junction with the caravan park service road we bear left to the main A165 road.

Crossing with caution, we now continue on the p.r.o.w. along the left side of the hedge, go over a sewage works access road and then cross the railway at (6). We cannot help but notice how peaceful this stretch of the walk is compared to the razzmatazz we encountered just a few miles earlier.

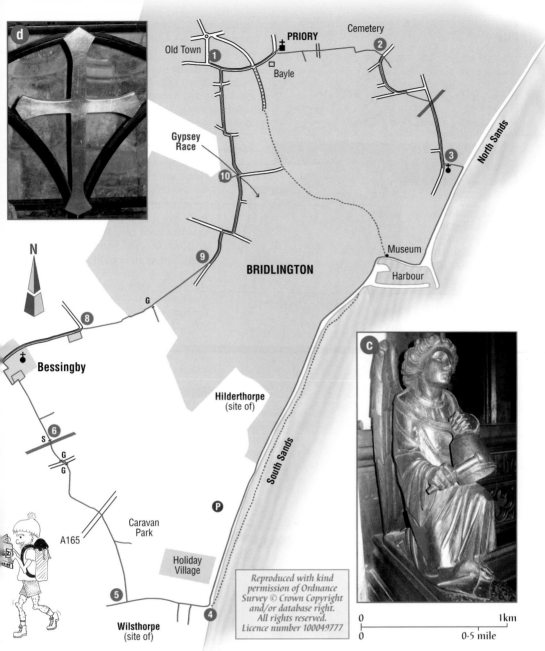

On the map: Old Town · ①; PRIORY; Cemetery; ②; Bayle; North Sands; ③; Gypsey Race; ⑩; BRIDLINGTON; Museum; Harbour; N; ⑨; G; ⑧; Bessingby; Hilderthorpe (site of); South Sands; ⑥; S; G; G; Caravan Park; A165; P; Holiday Village; ⑤; ④; Wilsthorpe (site of)

Reproduced with kind permission of Ordnance Survey © Crown Copyright and/or database right. All rights reserved. Licence number 100049777

0   1km
0   0·5 mile

On the other side of the rail line, the waymarked route stays by the field edge before we twist round three sides of a small copse on the edge of Bessingby. After this, we bear left and soon turn right (7) on the road through the settlement. It's only a small hamlet but we can view St Magnus Church to our right before continuing on the lane past Bessingby Hall Park on our left.

Where the lane bends sharp left (8) we continue straight ahead on a wide grassy footpath. After a while we pass a large allotment area and then soon reach the minor road (9) that runs through the adjacent industrial estate. For the final mile of the walk we will be going through the urban fringe of Bridlington and the suggested directions are:

Bearing slightly left on the service road, we continue to the roundabout in front of Morrisons, cross the main A165 road, turn right and then go first left down St John's Avenue. Almost immediately after the sharp right bend (10), we turn left down St John's Walk and spot the Gypsey Race on our left.

At the T-junction with Brett Street we go left to Brookland Road, turn right and carry on to High Street in Bridlington's Old Town. Turning left, and right, we arrive back at the car park from where we began.

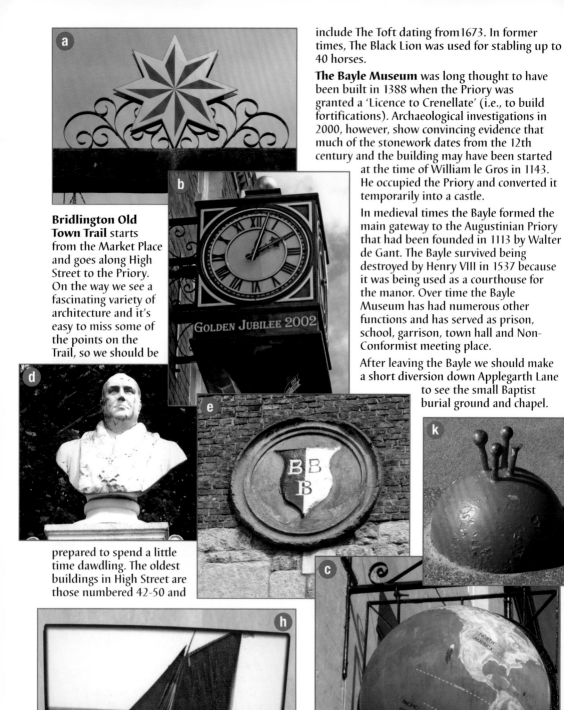

include The Toft dating from 1673. In former times, The Black Lion was used for stabling up to 40 horses.

The Bayle Museum was long thought to have been built in 1388 when the Priory was granted a 'Licence to Crenellate' (i.e., to build fortifications). Archaeological investigations in 2000, however, show convincing evidence that much of the stonework dates from the 12th century and the building may have been started at the time of William le Gros in 1143. He occupied the Priory and converted it temporarily into a castle.

In medieval times the Bayle formed the main gateway to the Augustinian Priory that had been founded in 1113 by Walter de Gant. The Bayle survived being destroyed by Henry VIII in 1537 because it was being used as a courthouse for the manor. Over time the Bayle Museum has had numerous other functions and has served as prison, school, garrison, town hall and Non-Conformist meeting place.

After leaving the Bayle we should make a short diversion down Applegarth Lane to see the small Baptist burial ground and chapel.

Bridlington Old Town Trail starts from the Market Place and goes along High Street to the Priory. On the way we see a fascinating variety of architecture and it's easy to miss some of the points on the Trail, so we should be prepared to spend a little time dawdling. The oldest buildings in High Street are those numbered 42-50 and

GOLDEN JUBILEE 2002

In bygone days this lifeboat was drawn by horses. On launching, a rope was placed between the boat carriage and this post. To act as a brake controlling the speed down the slip. This preventing injury to the animals and the lifeboat

landing port for shellfish, some of which is exported to Europe and even to Japan.

Much of the town's economy revolves around tourism and visitors are recorded as having bathed at Bridlington in 1770 but it was the arrival of the railway in 1846 that encouraged

Long. 0.11' W
Lat. 54.05' N

Bridlington Harbour

developed a mile from the Priory as a port, to be known as Burlington Quay, where the Gypsey Race enters the sea at Clough Hole. There was once a number of mills along the course of the Race, including some in Bridlington itself.

By the 13th century the Prior of Bridlington was responsible for the harbour's administration. Fishing was important in the Middle Ages and herring houses were located here in the 1530s.

In recent decades the severe decline in the stocks of North Sea herring and white fish has forced the fishing industry to concentrate on catching shellfish instead. In 2005 Bridlington was the U.K.'s most important

large numbers of people from the West Riding to make the journey to the seaside and as fishing was relatively poor in the summer months, fishermen began giving trips on their sailing cobles. One unusual feature of the harbour is the intermittent 'tidal spring' of fresh water which was discovered in 1811 by Benjamin Milne.

The three Bs (BBB) are the arms of the Manor of Bridlington (1663) and formerly the arms of Bridlington Priory. But what do they stand for? No-one is sure; there is no proven meaning so see if you can improve on 'Bright, Breezy and Bracing' as an advertising slogan for the East Riding's number one resort.

THIS TIDAL SPRING WAS DISCOVERED ON THE 5TH JULY, 1811, BY BENJAMIN MILNE, COLLECTOR OF CUSTOMS, BRIDLINGTON.

Bessingby has a number of 18th century cottages as well as Bessingby Hall which was rebuilt in 1807 for Harrington Hudson. A church existed in the early 12th century but **St Magnus Church** was built in the 1890s and replaced an earlier brick building that stood nearby.

WALK Y
Yapham

Map: Explorer 294
S.E.P.: St Martin's Church, Yapham
(789519)
Bus: 747 from Pocklington
Longer walk distance: 8.9 miles
Shorter walk alternative: 7.1 miles
Special interest:
Three villages

The route description starts from
St Martin's Church, Yapham,
where there is car parking space
adjacent to the village community
centre (1).

Leaving Yapham Church, we join
the road, turn right, bend right
again at the telephone box and
then left into High Bields.
Waymarks lead us between the
houses and to the gate at the edge
of the Mill Farm buildings (2).

From here we go down the first
field, do a left-right shimmy at
the boundary ditch and continue
northwards beside the hedge. There's a
right-left kink in the raised path before we
come to Bishop Wilton Beck at (3).

Here we go through the gate and, leaving
the main track, turn right along the stream.
It's now an easy stroll by the beck as it
bubbles its way round numerous mini-
meanders and we continue to Bishop
Wilton.

At the four-way road junction (4) we turn
right to walk into the village. Staying on the
left side of the beck, we go over the
crossroads and on to see St Edith's Church.
A very informative leaflet describes the
main features of this extremely attractive
Church and a visit is highly recommended.

When we leave the church and come back to the
road, we carry on to the primary school at the
end of the village, turn right to cross the beck and
go immediately left to locate the path at the
right-hand side of house number 78.

Rising slightly, we are led up and round the back
of the houses where the path becomes a track and
then a hard-surfaced road. This is Park Lane and
brings us to the crossroads at (5). We turn left
and follow the road for some 250m before
branching off left at the Minster Way fingerpost.

We face a steep rise along the field boundary as
we climb over the hummocks of the Wolds
escarpment. When we come to the gate on our
left (6), the p.r.o.w. turns right and we walk along
a terrace that is roughly 100m distant from the
hedge line at the top of the scarp. Needless to say,
on a good day the views across the Vale of York
are extensive.

We twist left where the path comes round to
meet the hedge, cross two stiles and are then led,
zigzag fashion, between fence and hedge to the
gate at (7). Bending left on to a wider track, and
staying right at the fork a little further on, we
reach the road in Great Givendale (8).

We turn left through the hamlet to the T-junction
and, using the church access path
straight ahead, we pay a brief
visit to St Ethelburga's Church
before returning to the road and
resuming the walk.

We go south in the direction of
Pocklington and have a good view
of the Givendale valley ponds to
our left.

At the next fingerpost (9) we
turn right off the road on to the
path at the edge of Brimlands
Wood. We soon switch from
right to left side of the wood
boundary and shortly after that
the path bends left.
It becomes wider
as we continue
towards the edge of
the chalk
escarpment.

About 100m before
the hedge in front
of us forces us to
swing left, a gap on
our right (10)
allows us to use
Open Access rights
on the scarp face.
Going through the
gap, the short walk
follows the path
bearing right and
going down the

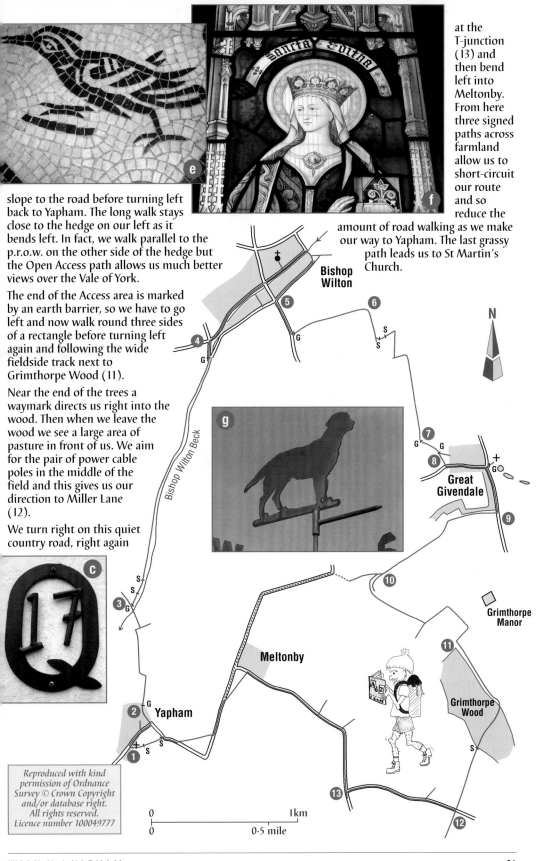

at the T-junction (13) and then bend left into Meltonby. From here three signed paths across farmland allow us to short-circuit our route and so reduce the amount of road walking as we make our way to Yapham. The last grassy path leads us to St Martin's Church.

slope to the road before turning left back to Yapham. The long walk stays close to the hedge on our left as it bends left. In fact, we walk parallel to the p.r.o.w. on the other side of the hedge but the Open Access path allows us much better views over the Vale of York.

The end of the Access area is marked by an earth barrier, so we have to go left and now walk round three sides of a rectangle before turning left again and following the wide fieldside track next to Grimthorpe Wood (11).

Near the end of the trees a waymark directs us right into the wood. Then when we leave the wood we see a large area of pasture in front of us. We aim for the pair of power cable poles in the middle of the field and this gives us our direction to Miller Lane (12).

We turn right on this quiet country road, right again

Bishop Wilton Beck

Bishop Wilton

Great Givendale

Grimthorpe Manor

Meltonby

Grimthorpe Wood

Yapham

N

0   1km
0   0·5 mile

Special Interest – Walk Y

Yapham 'homestead at the steep places' However, although the village is above the flat floor of the Vale of York, it is still a mile from the steep scarp edge of the Wolds

Meltonby not clear; perhaps 'farm of the meal-man' (one who deals in meal)

Great Givendale perhaps 'valley of the stream rich in fish' (or 'the rich valley'). The stream is small but there are old fish ponds

Bishop Wilton probably 'wild, uncultivated enclosure or farmstead'

Yapham is a scattered community and consists of three small hamlets. The village centre has the church and old school, now converted into the village hall. Yapham Mill (called Yapham Grange on the OS map) is located a mile to the south and is the site of the old flour mill. Meltonby lies to the north-east and is part of both the civil and the ecclesiastical parishes. Feoffee Lane runs roughly SW from the village over former common land and past the farm called Yapham Hall.

St Martin's Church has a Norman font but the church was largely rebuilt in 1777-78.

St Ethelburga's Church, Great Givendale is always open in daytime and has a Norman chancel arch. Ethelburga was the Christian wife of Edwin, King of Northumbria, and her faith led to his baptism into the Christian Church in AD 627.

The three ponds at Givendale are spring-fed and were restored by Richard Fuller for use as fish breeding ponds, although they are now seriously affected by sediment infilling.

St Edith's Church has a Norman chancel arch and south doorway, both of which are richly carved. The tower and spire date from the 15th century, while the eye-catching mosaic floor was inspired by a floor in the Vatican and was laid down in 1902. If time allows, try counting how many different birds you can identify from the mosaics.

Bishop Wilton was the site of a medieval manor house or summer 'palace' built and used by a succession of Archbishops of York in the Middle Ages. The palace complex was at the east end of the present village and was protected by a deep moat. It included a hall, library, chapel, living quarters, fish ponds and, it is thought, an adjacent deer park. The palace and all possessions were temporarily seized by the Crown after Archbishop Neville was forced to escape to mainland Europe after supporting the unpopular King Richard II.

Special Interest – Walk Z

The **Zigzag Plantation** lies on the Thorpe Hall Estate. The Hall was probably built about 1695 but was enlarged and remodelled in the 18th century. Then in the early 19th century Godfrey Bosville undertook a major landscaping of the grounds, digging the two ponds with their wooded islands and waterfalls, as well as erecting a number of ornamental garden buildings and creating a fine example of Regency estate design.

It is likely that the Zigzag Plantation was planted at this time. The OS Six Inch map of 1850 shows the Plantation, but interestingly the edge of the wood is less regular than it is today. There are a few more zigs, although they are curved rather than sharp-angled. Contemporary planning would have regarded a gentler, less regular boundary line more attractive to the eye.

Rudston Monolith is the largest single standing stone in Britain, being some 25ft (7.7m) high and about 6ft (1.8m) wide. It is composed of gritstone and must have been dragged some 10 miles from the nearest outcrop at Cayton Bay.

The monolith dates from the Neolithic Age and lies at the intersection of four Neolithic ditches that come into the village from north, east, south and west, so it is thought that this was probably the focus of religious ceremonies centuries before the coming of Christianity. Much later, Christians built their church on the same pagan site.

All Saints Church, Rudston was begun in Norman times but since then has seen much rebuilding. Winifred Holtby, the novelist best known for her *South Riding*, was born at Rudston House and is buried in the churchyard. Look carefully at the clock ...

A **Roman villa** found 0.5 mile to the SW of Rudston had fine mosaics and these can be seen in the Hull and East Riding Museum.

Boynton village and Burton Fleming, also in the valley of the Gypsey Race and visited on Walk **G**, afford an interesting example of the contrast between 'closed' and 'open' villages. When the fields of Boynton were enclosed in 1783, virtually all the land in the parish belonged to one man, Sir George Strickland. He had been able, therefore, to use his authority to

determine the development of the village. The old road near to the Gypsey Race had already been diverted to enlarge the Stricklands' park and ensure their privacy. Neither non-conformist chapel nor public house were allowed to be built in this 'closed' village. However, in spite of this, there was a woollen factory established by Sir George Strickland that operated in the 1760s but the venture was short-lived and Boynton remained small in population.

By contrast, in Burton Fleming where Sir George also owned land, he was only one of several landowners and after enclosure the settlement grew considerably in size. It was an 'open' village; Dissenters were numerous and by the mid-1800s there were three Methodist chapels as well as two public houses.

St Andrew's Church, Boynton contains the mausoleum of the Strickland family of Boynton Hall. William Strickland is said to have brought the first turkey to England in the 16th century and this explains why there are so many turkeys in the church. It's an interesting diversion to see how many you can count; a helpful hint is to remember that a turkey forms the crest of the Strickland family.

Caythorpe Gas Site was developed in 1992 to obtain natural gas from an underground rock formation. UK supplies of onshore natural gas are very limited and so this site is highly unusual. In 1997 three gas-driven electricity generators were installed to convert the gas into electricity and this was then fed into the National Grid. In 2002 gas production from a shallower rock formation was begun but by 2008 all operations had ceased.

However, planning permission has been given for drilling up to six new gas wells into the same 'reservoir' as the older wells. This reservoir lies some 1800m under-ground and is a layer of porous sandstone which contains the gas but from which the gas cannot escape (except through the borehole) because it is surrounded by other impermeable rocks. As might be expected, such development in a sensitive rural environment is highly controversial and has aroused strong local opposition. The surface location of the new wells will be about 0.75 mile west of the existing boreholes.

WALK Z
Zigzag Plantation near Rudston

Map: Explorer 301
S.E.P.:   St Andrew's Church, Boynton (137680)
Bus: 124 Bridlington-Driffield
Circular walk distance: **10.0 miles**
Shorter walk (uses bus or second car to
return to Boynton from Rudston):   **5.1 miles**
Special interest:
            Two Gypsey Race villages,
            Rudston monolith

a

Rudston takes its name from the monolith in
the churchyard. 'Rod' meant 'rood,
cross' and 'stan' referred to
the 'stone' used for the
cross. ('Rud' might also
mean 'red')

Boynton 'Bofa's farmstead'
Caythorpe 'Kari's village'

We start from St Andrew's
Church in Boynton (1).
Assuming we stand with our
backs to the church, we turn
right towards the village and go
quickly left and left again on the
bridleway that leads south and then SSE
towards Home Farm. Just before the farm the
Gypsey Race looks delightful as we cross the
stream and bend right, then left, around the
back of the barn to locate the brick steps on our
right leading up to the stile that directs us up
the valley side.

Climbing a second stile, we turn immediately
left, then right along the field edge to the end of
the fence before continuing up the gentle slope
to the Woldgate Roman Road at (2).

We go right on the road for 250m to another
bridleway that leads us off left between two
lines of trees. This brings us to Church Lane (3).

Crossing the road, we pick up the wide green
track offset to the left on the other side.

For the next 1.25 miles we have fine views in all
directions as we make our way, bearing right
when we join Hunger Hills Balk (4), to the
Roman Woldgate Road at (5).

A left turn on this road takes us to yet another
bridle track (6) where we turn right and follow
the hedge. We walk for about 600m before
leaving the fieldside and bearing left through a
small wood. Leaving the trees, we walk beside
the wood before swinging left. When we come
to the next wood at (7) we have
reached the Zigzag Plantation –
the reason for devising this walk
in the first place!

The route turns sharp right
and, staying outside the
plantation, we
are led down

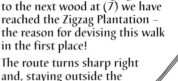

High
Caythorpe
15

14

North
Wood

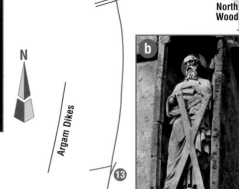

b

16

N

Argam Dikes

13

Rudston

Monolith

12   B1253

G

10   G

G   G

11

9   8

Zigzag
Plantation 7

Thorpe
Hall

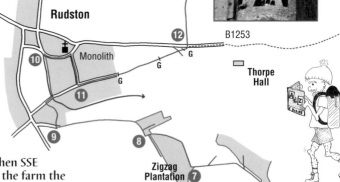

Woldga

G   Woldga

6

0   1km
0   0·5 mile

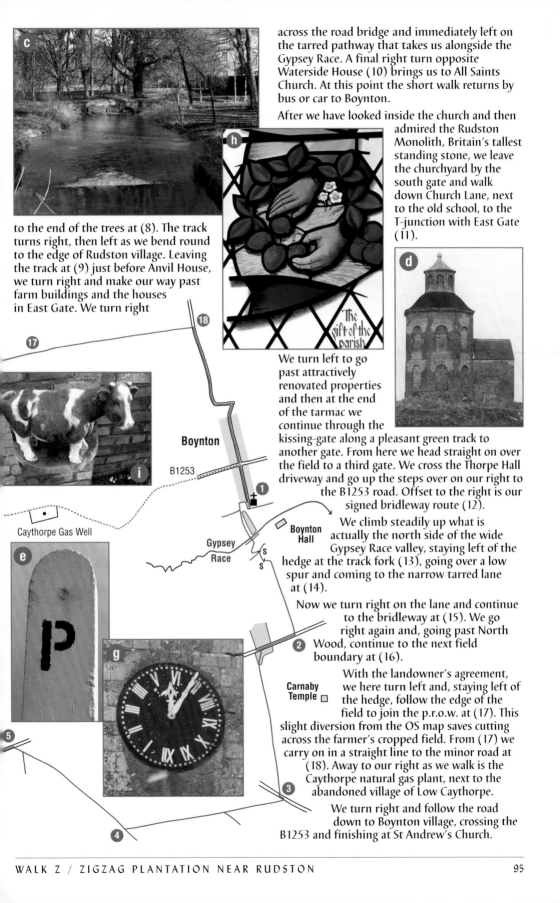

across the road bridge and immediately left on the tarred pathway that takes us alongside the Gypsey Race. A final right turn opposite Waterside House (10) brings us to All Saints Church. At this point the short walk returns by bus or car to Boynton.

After we have looked inside the church and then admired the Rudston Monolith, Britain's tallest standing stone, we leave the churchyard by the south gate and walk down Church Lane, next to the old school, to the T-junction with East Gate (11).

to the end of the trees at (8). The track turns right, then left as we bend round to the edge of Rudston village. Leaving the track at (9) just before Anvil House, we turn right and make our way past farm buildings and the houses in East Gate. We turn right

We turn left to go past attractively renovated properties and then at the end of the tarmac we continue through the kissing-gate along a pleasant green track to another gate. From here we head straight on over the field to a third gate. We cross the Thorpe Hall driveway and go up the steps over on our right to the B1253 road. Offset to the right is our signed bridleway route (12).

We climb steadily up what is actually the north side of the wide Gypsey Race valley, staying left of the hedge at the track fork (13), going over a low spur and coming to the narrow tarred lane at (14).

Now we turn right on the lane and continue to the bridleway at (15). We go right again and, going past North Wood, continue to the next field boundary at (16).

With the landowner's agreement, we here turn left and, staying left of the hedge, follow the edge of the field to join the p.r.o.w. at (17). This slight diversion from the OS map saves cutting across the farmer's cropped field. From (17) we carry on in a straight line to the minor road at (18). Away to our right as we walk is the Caythorpe natural gas plant, next to the abandoned village of Low Caythorpe.

We turn right and follow the road down to Boynton village, crossing the B1253 and finishing at St Andrew's Church.

Caythorpe Gas Well

Boynton

B1253

Gypsey Race

Boynton Hall

Carnaby Temple

TREASURE HUNT ANSWERS

WALK A

(a)	Cottages	(927409)
(b)	Baptist Chapel	(913368)
(c)	Cross base green	(913367)
(d)	The Gnu pub	(913367)
(e)	St Nicholas'	(912366)
(f)	Wind vane	(908367)
(g)	Catholic chapel	(899395)
(h)	School	(900394)
(i)	All Saints	(899395)

WALK B

(a/b)	St Leonard's	(152747)
(c)	Bench	(153749)
(d)	Boundary	(168749)
(e)	RSPB Centre	(197738)
(f)	Jaw Bones	(192724)
(g)	St Michael's	(191721)
(h/i/j)	Houses on main road	

WALK C

(a/b)	St Mary's	(966655)
(c)	Easterby	(987657)
(d)	Cottam Grange	(988656)
(e)	Fence notice	(989656)
(f)	Derelict Church	(994649)
(g)	W W II remains	(994649)
(h)	Site of Cottam	(994649)
(i)	Notice	(973635/977643)
(j)	Marbled White in Dale	

WALK D (MAP)

(a)	North Landing	(238722)
(b)		
(c)	Old Lighthouse	(250708)
(d)	High Stacks	(258704)
(e)	Sewerby Rocks	(210689)
(f)	Sewerby Hall	(204691)
(g)	Flamb' Castle	(227703)

WALK D (TRAIL)

(a)	Pub	(226706)
(b)	Memorial	(226706)
(c)	North Landing	(239720)
(d)	Toposcope	(254707)
(e)	by Lighthouse	(254707)
(f)	nr S. Landing	(233693)
(g)	Lifeboat Centre	(231692)
(h)	Danes' Dyke	(216694)
(i)	Dotto Train Sewerby	
(j/k/l)	St Oswald's	(226701)

WALK E (MAP)

(a)	The Clocks	(781414)
(b)	Road junction	(804426)
(c)	Rook House	(804424)
(d)	Outside Church	(821389)
(e/f)	All Saints	(821389)
(g)	Kingfisher pub	(816388)
(h)	Black Horse	(782408)
(i)	Peep O Day	(782410)

WALK E (TRAIL)

(a)	Bielby Chapel	(789437)
(b/c)	St Edmund's	(781413)
(d)	Dial Cottage	(777416)
(e)	Dial House Fm	(773425)

WALK F

(a/b)	St Mary's	(875592)
(c)	Farmers Arms	(875591)
(d)	House name	(874590)
(e)	'Wayside'	(874589)
(f)	Roadside	(856576)
(g)	by gate	(865593)
(h)	Millington Glebe Farm	(873593)

WALK G (MAP)

(a)	Willy Howe	(062724)
(b)	Meteorite Mon	(038721)
(c)	Gypsey Race	(047727)

WALK G (TRAIL)

(a)	St Cuthbert's	(084723)
(b)	Hogpenny	(084722)
(c)	Chapel	(083721)
(d/e)	Road junction	(083720)
(f)	Pub	(052700)
(g)	Road junction	(049700)
(h)	All Saints	(049702)
(i)	Anvil Pub	(047729)
(j)	All Saints	(046725)
(k)	Front Street	(045726)
(l)	Caravan Park	(078733)

WALK H

(a/b)	St Mary's	(882555)
(c)	September Cott	(882555)
(d)	Main street	(882555)
(e)	Final Frontier	(881556)
(f)	Strawberry pick	(880542)
(g)	Huggate Dykes	(859559)
(h)	Cross base	(875558)
(i)	Village well	(883552)

WALK I

(a)	St John's	(733510)
(b)	Bridge Cottage	(732508)
(c)	Hall Farm	(722496)
(d)	Lych Gate	(720497)
(e)	Marker stone	(706504)
(f)	Pinfold Cottage	(707530)
(g)	Mill Bungalow	(724515)
(h)	School	(728511)

WALK J

(a)	All Hallows	(998368)
(b)	No 12 Kirk Lane	(997369)
(c)	Ferguson Fawsitt	(998371)
(d)	The Barrel pub	(999371)
(e)	Black Mill	(021390)
(f)	Nursery	(030377)
(g)	White Hall Fm	(039372)
(h)	Orchard	(041369)
(i)	Risby Park sign	(018353)

WALK K

(a)	Car park	(410158)
(b)	Visitor Centre	(416158)
(c)	Sea defences	(422142)
(d)	Weather station	(398106)
(e)	Moth caterpillars	(398106)
(f)	Low Lighthouse	(402112)
(g)	Highland cattle	(409120)
(h)	Notice on gate	(418151)

WALK L

(a/b/c)	St Mary's	(997468)
(d)	House name	(997469)
(e)	Wayside seat	(993474)
(f)	Old Macdonalds	(972481)
(g/h)	Lund centre	(970481)
(i)	All Saints, Lund	(972481)
(j)	Before Kilnwick	(996494)
(k/l/m)	All Saints	(997495)
(n)	Grave, St Mary's	(022497)
(o)	Beswick Mill	(015488)
(p)	Main Street	(012484)
(q)	Front Street	(998473)

WALK M

(a)	St Margaret's	(830518)
(b)	Woodgate Farm	(835527)
(c)	'D' Gait Post	(847538)
(d)	Woodhouse Lane	(811507)
(e)	Corner View	(813514)
(f)	Orchard House	(830516)
(g)	Town Farm	(831518)
(h)	by Church	(829518)

WALK N

(a)	Crane	(029572)
(b)	Blue Bell pub	(028573)
(c)	No. 47 Westgate	(054587)
(d/e)	High Street	(055594)
(f)	Middle Street	(056592)
(g)	Springrise	(065561)
(h)	Copper Hall Farm	(063548)
(i)	Rose Cottage	(044552)
(j)	Londesborough	(043553)

WALK O (ROUTE MAP)

(a/b)	Promenade	(344279)
(c)	Hull Road	(339280)
(d)	Road junction	(316284)
(e)	'K Fresh' Eggs	(310290)
(f)	Drive to house	(309290)
(g)	All Saints	(291296)
(h)	Rectory Road	(289300)

WALK O
(SPECIAL INTEREST)

(a)	St Mary	(343280)
(b)	St Mary's	(311287)
(c)	All Saints	(305320)
(d)	Cliff erosion	

WALK P

(a)	Notice board	(835568)
(b)	Deep Dale	(823556)
(c)	Main Street	(807586)
(d)	Path to church	(808586)
(e/f)	All Saints	(808586)
(g)	Cross	(812584)
(h)	Pains. Hall	(813584)
(i)	Recent plantation	(824583)

WALK Q

(a)	B. Agnes Hall	(103632)
(b)	Path to church	(102632)
(c)	St Martin's (Burton Agnes)	(102632)
(d)	St John's Well	(095617)
(e)	St John's Church	(092616)
(f)	Lowthorpe	(083604)
(g)	St Martin's (Lowthorpe)	(079608)
(h)	Quintin Bottom	(076620)
(i)	All Saints	(064644)
(j)	East Street	(066644)

WALK R

(a)	Cottage	(942297)
(b)	Churchyard	(944301)
(c)	Plane in field	(937315)
(d)	Weedley Farm	(956322)
(e)	Roadside M.S.	(956321)
(f)	Pheasants sign	(964291)
(g)	Rowley Manor	(976326)
(h/i)	St Peter's	(976326)

WALK S (MAP)

(a)	Old Rectory	(155456)
(b/c)	St Lawrence	(154456)
(d)	Seaton	(163466)
(e)	AA plaque	(164467)
(f)	Farberry	(196475)
(g)	Southorpe Lodge	(198467)

WALK S (TOWN TRAIL)

(a)	Quaker Cottage	(199476)
(b)	Rose & Crown	(200476)
(c)	No. 13 Mosaic	(201476)
(d)	No. 14 Museum	(202476)
(e)	No. 15 Museum	(202476)
(f)	No. 16 Folly	(203476)
(g)	No.9 Skate Park	(205479)
(h)	Promenade	(209482)
(i)	No.4 Promenade	(209482)
(j)	Guest House	(209480)
(k)	No. 3 Beacon	(209479)
(l)	No. 19 Gardens	(207478)

WALK T (MAP)

(a)	Churchyard	(208264)
(b)	next to Church	(208264)
(c)	Gas plant	(179253)
(d)	Old CG Station	(167260)
(e)	Old Chapel	(166266)
(f)	Entering Paull	(166267)
(g)	The Forge	(220263)
(h)	Roadside M.S.	(218263)

WALK T (TOWN TRAIL)

(a)	House No. 42	(186285)
(b)	New Hall	(189285)
(c)	Queen's Head	(189286)
(d)	Town Hall	(189287)
(e)	St Augustine's	(188288)
(f)	Market Hill	(188288)
(g)	Street name	(189289)
(h)	Old almshouses	(189289)
(i)	King's Head	(189288)
(j)	Old Chapel	(190288)
(k)	Kilnsea Cross	(190288)
(l)	Shakespeare pub	(191286)

WALK U

(a)	Gorman Castle	(791586)
(b)	Farm driveway	(786585)
(c)	Under 5s Nursery	(773578)
(d/e)	St Andrew's	(773579)
(f)	Low Hall	(772581)
(g/h)	Gilderbeck House	(786600)
(i)	Mt Pleasant Farm	(811592)
(j)	Old Chapel	(8115492)

WALK V (MAP)

(a)	No 114 Hailgate	(749281)
(b)	On Kilpin Road	(759274)
(c)	B'ferry Bridge	(733263)
(d)	Black Swan	(718280)
(e)	Box Tree Farm	(716281)
(f)	Barley House Fm	(720297)

WALK V (TOWN TRAIL)

(a/b)	Minster	(748282)
(c)	Corn Market	(747282)
(d/e/f)	Market Place	(749282)
(g)	The Ashes	(749281)
(h)	Folly over moat	(749281)
(i)	Catholic Church	(745280)
(j)	War Memorial	(748283)
(k)	Bowman's pub	(749284)
(l)	Wellington pub	(749284)
(m)	Co-op store	(749284)
(n)	Methodist Ch	(750284)
(o)	Rodeo	(749283)
(p)	Butcher's shop	(749283)

WALK W

(a)	Chariot site	(935591)
(b/c)	St Nicholas'	(933590)
(d)	Corner building	(934590)
(e)	Road crossing	(946580)
(f)	Sykes Mon	(957618)
(g)	opp Sykes Mon	(957618)
(h)	Main Street	(932591)

WALK X (MAP)

(a/b/c/d/e)	All at Bridlington Priory	(177680)

WALK X (TOWN TRAIL)

(a)	Westgate	(171676)
(b/c)	High Street	(173679)
(d)	Kirkgate	(176679)
(e)	Bayle Museum	(176679)
(f)	Beaconsfield	(189671)
(g)	Arcades	(188669)
(h)	Maritime Mus	(186665)
(i)	Milne's Spring	(185666)
(j)	Slipway	(183664)
(k)	Crazy Golf	(181663)
(l)	Flagstone	(180662)

WALK Y

(a/b)	St Martin's	(789521)
(c)	Main Street	(796550)
(d)	Mosquito Cottage	(798552)
(e/f)	St Edith's	(798552)
(g)	Wilton Park	(799550)
(h)	Little Manor Fm	(811538)
(i)	St Ethelburga's	(813539)
(j)	Ivy Cottage	(796524)

WALK Z

(a/b)	St Andrew's	(136680)
(c)	Gypsey Race	(137677)
(d)	Carnaby Temple	(114666)
(e)	Woldgate Road	(118663)
(f/g/h)	All Saints	(098677)
(i)	Eastgate	(099675)
(j)	Eastgate	(098675)

POVERTY

LET'S END IT

'You are changing lives for the better through the contribution you are making.'

Delroy Powell, Pastor and Christian Aid supporter, England

christian **aid**

POVERTY

Visit **www.christianaid.org.uk** to find out how you can help.